A Book to Sit With

Inspiration & Guidance for the Journey

For Julie —

With my love,

Doris Wedige

doriswedige@gmail.com

A BOOK TO SIT WITH

INSPIRATION & GUIDANCE FOR THE JOURNEY

DORIS WEDIGE

COGENT PUBLISHING NY

Published by Cogent Publishing NY
Imprint of The Whitson Group, Inc.
3 Miller Road, Putnam Valley, NY 10579
www.cogent-publishing.com

Manufactured in the United States of America
First Edition

ISBN: 978-0-925776-40-2
1 2 3 4 5 6 7 — 19 18 17 16 15

6-1-2018

This book is dedicated to all
who yearn to live in the Way of Love.

Julie,
My friend Doris created this
lovely book. I thought you might
enjoy. Reading one page a day
seems to be a nice way to go.
I ASK one favor. If you like
the book, send Doris a note
to let her know. This is my way
of loving two friends with one
gift!! Love you!! Karl

CONTENTS

INTRODUCTION

IMAGINE THAT YOU HAVE BEEN allotted a little plot of ground and are creating the most beautiful garden that you can possibly imagine. You are the gardener that tends to the seeds, the soil, and the environment that are the necessary elements for the garden to flourish. Inspired thoughts are the seeds of potential, all that makes up your life is the garden and your faithful spirit is the loving atmosphere that nourishes the garden as it grows. *Live Beautifully: A Book to Sit With* is a tool that inspires and guides you on your Journey of Transformation as you become a Master Gardener capable of realizing your highest potential.

My journey began one warm, sunny day while on a camping trip with family and friends. I was alone, hiking in the woods, when my life was suddenly changed. I heard a voice. It was a big, strong, kind, masculine voice. It did not come from a person. It said only two words. "Live Beautifully." I was struck by awe and am at a loss even now for words to describe the experience. I had never heard a voice come from anything but a person. I spent the next few days at camp in an inner, silent wonder.

I had no idea what this voice had asked me to do, but as the days passed by I began to realize that the message was an invitation... an invitation for me to 'birth' a book. I had no idea what it was to be about, and was uncertain as to what I was getting myself into. Just as I always known that I would marry and have children, I had always known too that one day I would write a book. And so, back home from our camping trip, while riding on my bike down a country road, I found myself shouting, "Yes, I choose to Live Beautifully! Plant the seed in me and I will bring forth this potential in my garden!" I smiled joyfully as I pedaled along feeling the strength and enthusiasm that followed my acceptance.

Sometimes I have wondered, "Why me?" I seem to lack the normal credentials to write a book. Although I have loved journaling since I was a little girl, I didn't major in English in college and have never even written a magazine article. But I think that is exactly why me. Because of my lack of credentials, my biggest 'talent' was to simply sit down and wait to see what would come.

Live Beautifully is what came. As I journaled my thoughts I soon came to realize that our minds basically move between two realms—one, the lower realm is a negative mindset that is in need of transformation—doubt, shame, unworthiness, disorder, worry and anxiety are all in this lower realm. The second mindset, the Upper Realm is where Self-Worth, Self-Respect, Beauty, Authenticity and Compassion are the norm, and it is to the Upper Realm that my personal Journey of Transformation lead me. I found that to Live Beautifully is to be aware of the choices that are available each day, and to take steps into living more fully with Love in the Upper Realm.

The Live Beautifully Journey is available to those who find that their minds are plagued with much falseness and that their bodies and spirits are a reflection of the same. It is a source of support for those who have made the choice to take responsibility for their own self-healing.

The book begins with lists of what takes place in your mind, body and spirit when you are in the Upper Realm or lower realm. Refer to these as your journey progresses. Add the words that describe your personal experience in these two realms. These lists are followed by Reflections which are excerpts from my personal journals. I share my Journey to awaken you to what you may or may not yet be willing to see in yourself. I hope that you will choose to be Compassionate towards me and then, with Awareness, be the same for yourself.

The message I share with you, "Live Beautifully," contains a second invitation: a call to wake up to a new way of living. It is an invitation to begin your journey; a Journey of Transformation from the lower realm where you have been controlled by fear, to the Upper Realm where you create with Love. It is time to embark on your Live Beautifully Journey, to choose to nurture yourself with Acceptance and Compassion as you make the choice to heal yourself from within. Healing is available as a natural consequence of choosing to align yourself with Love.

This is an invitation to you that requires a response. Make the inner choice and say "Yes, I choose to Live Beautifully! Plant the seed in me and I will bring forth this potential in my garden!" I open my heart and my arms to each and every one of you that join me on this trail. Thank you. Thank you. Thank you. Your courage and tenacity will change you and change the world.

DORIS WEDIGE

Realms of Mind, Body & Spirit

Upper Realm Mind

OUR PERCEPTION WHEN WE PUT FAITH IN BELIEFS THAT
ARE BASED ON LOVE AND THUS OUR THOUGHTS ARE OF:

SELF-LOVE

SELF-WORTH

SELF-HONOR

SELF-RESPECT

SELF-ESTEEM

AWARENESS

Lower Realm Mind

OUR PERCEPTION WHEN WE PUT FAITH IN BELIEFS
THAT ARE BASED ON FEAR AND SEPARATION AND
THUS OUR THOUGHTS ARE OF:

JUDGMENT

REJECTION

UNWORTHINESS

DOUBT

REGRET

SCARCITY

GUILT

BLAME

SHAME

SEPARATION

(Mental Health)

Upper Realm Body

Our physical experiences that are
a reflection of choices that are
based on beliefs in Truth and Love:

Unity

Creativity

Generosity

Beauty

Vitality/Abundance

Authenticity

Order

Lower Realm Body

Our physical experiences that are a
reflection of choices that are based
on beliefs of fear and separation:

DISORDER

INDECISIVENESS

LUST/GREED

LAZINESS/COMPLACENCY/INDIFFERENCE

JEALOUSY/ENVY

WANTING

SUPERIORITY/INFERIORITY/SEPARATION

(Physical Health)

Upper Realm Spirit

Our spiritual experience when we put
faith in beliefs that are based on Love:

Gratitude

Enthusiasm

Joyfulness

Optimism

Peacefulness

Serenity

Compassion

Acceptance

Lower Realm Spirit

Our spiritual experience when we put
faith in beliefs that are based on fear
and separation:

NERVOUSNESS/ANXIETY

WORRY/TENSION

RESENTMENT

UNCERTAINTY

ANGER

(Spiritual Health)

JOURNALING FOR TRANSFORMATION

I see... I accept... I relinquish... I dream of...
With peace and love I intend to... I am grateful...

JOURNALING FOR TRANSFORMATION HAS BEEN the cornerstone of my healing Journey. It is a tool that I use to shift from the place where I am suffering—the lower realm—to a place where I find peace—the Upper Realm. I sit with a cup of coffee and journal each morning in devotion to growing into my full potential of being a Master Gardener. Using journaling as a tool, I seek to align myself more fully with the Upper Realm, the place where I am healed.

This healing process begins with Awareness of feelings. The Upper Realm feels good. The lower realm feels anywhere from downright horrible to just mildly irritating. The parts that are irritating are the places that are ready for change. These tend to be the things that are 'on my mind.' I think of this healing process as pulling back layers of an onion. There are many layers of the lower realm to deal with. But each day I just choose one layer, the thinnest outer layer. I leave the deep inner layers alone. They will come to the surface to be dealt with at a later time. Day by day I deal with one layer, one choice.

One of the biggest challenges in getting out of the lower realm is to stay focused on your own self-healing. It is so easy to make the error of thinking that the obvious solution to a problem is for other people to change their ways. Awareness followed by anger, resentment, blame or defensiveness is just a lower realm response to a lower realm situation. Although it is indeed true that we all have work to do in aligning ourselves with the Upper Realm, we all need to focus on our own individual work.

I've come to know that anything that bothers me is a 'place' where I have work to do. Each of the reflections in this book include a short Journaling for Transformation process. But if you feel inclined to use the process on your own, here is an explanation of the steps:

Step 1: Begin to journal with the intent to gain Awareness in a situation that is irritating you. This can be anything from the mess in a closet to the stressful situations with your relatives. Write about what is irritating you with the intent to discover a lower realm choice that you are making. This is always a seeking about you. Over and over you must resist the temptation to react like a detective in a crime scene. You must resist the temptation to analyze the situation in an attempt figure out what others are doing in the lower realm.

Write '*I see...*' and continue to journal seeking Awareness of your own lower realm choices: mind, body and/or spirit. The reflections in this book are the 'I see' step. Do your best to watch out for feeling justified. Awareness followed by a lower realm response is usually accompanied by a sense of being justified. For example, you might feel justified in a lower realm choice to blame someone else or to respond to life with worry or victimization. A sense of feeling justified doesn't follow an Upper Realm choice. We don't experience a sense of being justified in being Compassionate, Faithful or Loving. Awareness followed by believing you are justified is an indication that you are staying stuck in a rut in the lower realm. Awareness followed by Acceptance is the necessary leap of faith that creates the bridge from the lower to the Upper Realm. Continue writing until you reach the point of Awareness and Acceptance.

Step 2: When you are ready to cross the bridge to the Upper Realm write '*I accept...*' and put it into words. Make sure to write it all out in complete sentences. In this moment of Acceptance realize that you made choices based on lower realm beliefs as they blocked your capacity to be aware of an Upper Realm choice. All that triggers your lower realm choices are simply your personal limits of your capacity to respond to life with Love due to an illness of your mind.

Humanity is literally ill in our minds. When we put faith in the false thoughts that result from this illness, we 'sin.' The Greek meaning of sin is 'to miss the mark.' We merely make the error of putting faith in fear instead of Love. We 'miss the mark.' Love is the mark. Forgiveness is the open invitation to return to Love. Acceptance is the first step of embracing the invitation to return to Love. This step of the transformative process is a powerful shift in your perception from fear to Love.

Step 3: In seeing the falseness of the situation, you are ready to make the choice to relinquish it all. Write '*I relinquish...*' and declare an intent to let go of all that does not serve you. This can be a letting go of old beliefs, old habits, or old pain that you carry in your energy field. This is a clearing of the slate. This is the act of being forgiving. This is the 'let it go' stage of the process. This is the healing step. This is a shift into healing yourself by Loving yourself. This step cleans up the old blockages; it purifies your body and your Garden of the consequences of your past errors. You can pay off your errors by putting in the time to release karmic debt or you can decide to accept the gift of forgiveness. Please know that you are worthy of forgiveness.

Step 4: After letting go of what has tethered you to the lower realm, your mind is then an open expanse for receiving Inspiration for living in the Upper Realm. Write '*I dream of...*' and follow up with a flow of Inspirations for creating your life with Love. Relax and let the ink flow as you dream of the most beautiful life you can possibly imagine. Dream of a new way of being. Let your imagination soar. Open yourself to being inspired to Live Beautifully. This is the opportunity to page through the seed catalog of your life's potential.

Step 5: This is the point where you must exercise your free will. You can either honor the Inspiration by intending it with Peace and Love or you can go back to your old ways. Write '*With peace and love I intend to...*' and declare a statement of intent. This is the act of choosing and planting a seed in your Garden.

Step 6: The final step in the Journaling for Transformation process is to express the gratitude that naturally flows when you have taken a step up on your Journey. Write '*I am grateful...*' and give thanks for the healing, for the Guidance and for what is to be. This is the act of choosing to nourish your Garden with an atmosphere of Gratitude that flows from your heart. This is your opportunity to be a loving spirit that brings Life to the seed of potential that you have planted in your Garden.

I hope that you will join me in my daily devotion to Journaling for Transformation. In doing so we each take another step on the Journey towards being Master Gardeners, those who Live Beautifully, those who create with Love in Union with All.

Journaling for Transformation: *I see* that an illness has infected humanity and thus we suffer: mind, body and spirit... *I accept* the responsibility of my own self-healing... *I relinquish* being a victim... *I dream of* taking a step on my Journey each and every day... *With peace and love I intend to* heal by Journaling for Transformation... *I am grateful* that I am becoming a Master Gardener, I am.

* You are invited to visit www.livebeautifully.us for more tools to use on your journey.
* Throughout this book words that convey Awareness of the Upper Realm have been capitalized.

REFLECTIONS ON THE JOURNEY

Oh God...
Once again, here I am.
Another day.
Another beautiful day.
Please bless me with a healed mind, a healed body, and a healed spirit.
Please bless me with awareness of my heart, the compass that guides me.
Please bless me with the wisdom to honor what I love.
Please bless me with awareness of guidance.
Please bless me with the wisdom to honor guidance.
Please bless my creations this day.
Please bless me with Grace so that I might be a Light in this world.
Thank you. Thank you. Thank you.
Amen.

The greatest achievement was at first and for a time a dream.
The oak sleeps in the acorn, the bird waits in the egg,
and in the highest vision of the soul a waking angel stirs.
Dreams are the seedlings of realities.
JAMES ALLEN

*R*EFLECTIONS ON JOINING THE DANCE… My whole body smiles as I gaze up at a young oak tree against a pale blue morning sky. The leaves flutter in a joyful dance. So many beautiful shades of green backlit by the rising sun. What mesmerizes me is the movement. The Dance of Life. Bonfires have the same effect on me. The same dance, just a different form.

As I look around my backyard I see that the cattails have joined in the Dance… My rooster crows from his coop like a square dance caller announcing the beginning of a new dance. "Rise and shine everyone!" he seems to say, "Wake up and join the Dance!"

The birds chatter and my kitties' ears dance a dance all their own in union with it all. A flock of sand hill cranes just took flight off in the distance. Their ancient calls stir a knowing deep within me that I cannot name.

Oh, how sweet is the promise of a new day, another chance to participate fully in the Dance of Life.

Finish each day and be done with it.
You have <u>done</u> what you could.
Some blunders and absurdities no doubt crept in;
forget them as soon as you can.
Tomorrow is a new day.
You shall begin it serenely and with too high a spirit
to be encumbered with your old nonsense.
RALPH WALDO EMERSON

I INTEND TO JOIN MORE FULLY IN THE DANCE.

I accept that I have not always joined fully in the Dance… *I relinquish* fears that hold me back from pursuing my passions… *I dream of* dancing… *With peace and love I intend to* fully engage in a lifetime of Joy… *I am grateful* for the fabulous creation that I am a part of, *I am.*

Everyone thinks of changing the world,
but no one thinks of changing himself.
LEO TOLSTOY

*R*EFLECTIONS ON CHANGES... I feel my life shifting. There are changes on the horizon. Things are happening that look like losses, but that may just be my limited perspective. Maybe they aren't losses but things that need to move out of the way for the new to come in. When we intend for something new to come into our lives, we need to accept that change is inevitable. "Nothing changes if nothing changes."

My dear friend called this week and offered a bit of wisdom. She said our habits are like paths through the forest. If we want to let go of old ways, we must blaze a new trail. And then keep taking that new trail. If we leave the old trail alone, it will soon grow over with vegetation and become a thing of the past. But, if we occasionally take the old path, it will remain open and continue to be a part of our life.

I want to make a new path. Not just for myself but for others to use as well. I want to mark the trail with signs that lead the people who come to this trail; signs of direction, signs of inspiration, signs of encouragement. Walk with me my friends as we blaze a new trail. Hand in hand with the courage to live in a new way. Let's choose the path of Love, Peace, and Compassion. Let's choose to live with Grace.

We will leave behind the old path that was plagued with so many nasties—fear, doubt, indecision, neglect, worry and judgment. We will leave those on the old path to be overgrown and forgotten. It's a new day. I extend my hand to you my friend; please join me on the Live Beautifully Path.

A journey of a thousand miles
begins with a single step.
CHINESE PROVERB

I INTEND TO BLAZE A NEW TRAIL.

I accept that I must change if I want something different in my life... *I relinquish* fears of leaving the familiar behind... *I dream of* having the courage and tenacity to blaze a new trail... *With peace and love I intend to* Live Beautifully... *I am grateful* for this new path and for the many people who are on it, *I am.*

It is not the strongest or the most intelligent who will survive
but those who can best manage change.
CHARLES DARWIN

℞EFLECTIONS ON OUR BLOOMING... Like the flora 114 million years ago, we are alive and beautiful growing quite nicely in the shadows of our world. At some point in time the plants changed, a new aspect of creation came forth. Flowers began to emerge. First just one, then another, and finally an all out explosion of creation.

Has humanity experienced the blooming of a few souls? Is it time in evolution for a widespread blooming? Is the world ready to bring forth a new aspect of creation? Are we ready to step out of the darkness and into the Light? In doing so, will we create the circumstances necessary for an entirely new aspect of humanity to bloom?

At one point the earth opened up to a transformation. Roses, lilies, orchids, and daises were the result of this opening. They were beautiful new creations.

Can you feel a new aspect of humanity within you ready to burst forth? Are you ready to bloom in a new way? Have the courage to accept change, to step out of the dark and into the Light so that the conditions will be favorable for your flowering, a new and glorious flowering of humanity.

Man's mind,
once stretched by a new idea,
never regains its original dimensions.
OLIVER WENDELL HOLMES SR.

I INTEND TO EVOLVE AND BLOOM.

I accept the way things are... *I relinquish* fears that block me from embracing change... *I dream of* blooming into an exquisite creation... *With peace and love I intend to* have the courage to step out of the darkness... *I am grateful* for making the choice to Live Beautifully, *I am.*

*R*EFLECTIONS ON STRENGTH... I remember an early spring day. I had gone on a walk outdoors. I was intrigued by the effects of the long cold Wisconsin winter season. The paved road that passes in front of our house was pocked with potholes and upheaved in long lengths down its center. It had not fared well against the effects of the elements.

I turned off the road and as I emerged from an opening of trees, I was captivated by the beauty of the tall grasses that danced in the wind before me. They were bending and swaying amidst the powerful forces of the brisk wind. How had they survived the same harsh winter that crumbled the pavement of the road? These simple shafts of prairie grasses, so seemingly fragile, lived a life of beauty and grace amidst so much turmoil.

It leads me to ponder my concept of strength. Is there more strength in the rigidness of the concrete or is there more strength in the flexibility of a shaft of grass? I saw myself reflected in these elements. Like the road I have tried to stand strong against the harshness of life. Despite my mental strength, just like the road, I crumbled. My body has been wrought with pain; my back is out of alignment. It has buckled just like the road.

I want to be like the beautiful grasses. Flowing with what is. No attempt to stand strong against life's harshness. Just being with what is. Moving with what is. Living with powerful nonresistance. 'Live Beautifully' has new meaning for me. Live Beautifully means to have the strength to lovingly flow with what is.

I INTEND TO HAVE THE STRENGTH TO ACCEPT THINGS AS THEY ARE.

I accept that I have mistakenly sought strength in being rigid... *I relinquish* fears of being weak... *I dream of* being free from rigidness... *With peace and love I intend to* live with acceptance... *I am grateful* for the effects of flowing with what is, *I am.*

*R*EFLECTIONS ON A CONTROLLED BURN... On my way into town I descend a hill. The elevated road offers me a great vantage point to appreciate the beauty of the valley and the creek that runs through it.

About a month ago someone did a controlled burn. The entire landscape was changed to a large expanse of black. I wondered what the future would hold for this beautiful natural area. Would it come back a cesspool of weeds? We live on a similar area of land and I considered just for a moment that we too could do a controlled burn. But I quickly dismissed the thought for fear of what the result would be. I felt better just leaving things as they were. Who knows what kind of troubles doing something like that might entail!

It's a month later and on my trips to town I look out at the area where they did the burn and see a beautiful expanse of lush green. Absolutely gorgeous green. There is not one indication of the burn that happened just a month ago. The whole area looks fresh and renewed.

As I drove past last night I pondered the thought of doing a controlled burn on my own self. I pondered what it would be like to burn away my past. What would it be like to start with a clean slate? If I cleared away my past, would I too experience a burst of new growth? Would it open me up to new possibilities? How many of us would rather keep the status quo than risk the uncertainty of something different?

I'm ready for a controlled burn. I'm ready to start anew. I'm ready to burn away the past and let it be nourishment for the rich soil from which my future will grow.

The best skill at cards is knowing when to discard.
BALTASAR GRACIÁN

I INTEND TO SAY YES TO A CLEAN SLATE.

I accept that it can seem scary to release the past... *I relinquish* fears of not having excuses for my shortcomings if I were to burn away my past... *I dream of* a fire burning within me... *With peace and love I intend to* allow my past to burn away... *I am grateful* for a new day with fertile ground for new growth, *I am.*

Earth and sky, woods and fields,
lakes and rivers, the mountain and the sea,
are excellent schoolmasters,
and teach some of us more than we can ever learn from books.
JOHN LUBBOCK

*R*EFLECTIONS ON BEING FLUID... There is so much that I could learn about life from a babbling brook. They are a constantly changing flow. There are aspects that are relatively constant: the banks along its edges, the rocks and pebbles dispersed at its floor, the plants whose roots hold tight to the earth while their form is in a beautiful dance undulating with the flow of the water. There are bubbles that seem to come from nowhere, floating and dodging downstream, coming and going, no permanence.

Babbling brooks are nature's state of joy: a beautiful flow, a dance, a life of least resistance. The water doesn't map out a predetermined course; it just flows along on its journey. It doesn't worry about where it's been or where it's going.

I intend to live like the babbling brook. I intend to accept the impermanence of things. I intend to live in the Flow. I intend to be a reflection of Light.

The great sea has set me in motion.
Set me adrift,
And I move as a weed in the river.
The arch of sky
And mightiness of storms
Encompasses me,
And I am left
Trembling with joy.
UVAVNUK

I INTEND TO LIVE IN THE FLOW.

I accept where I have been... *I relinquish* fears of where I am going... *I dream of* living in the Flow... *With peace and love I intend to* be a reflection of Light... *I am grateful* for letting go of resistance, *I am.*

The best lightning rod for your protection is your own spine.
RALPH WALDO EMERSON

*R*EFLECTIONS ON SAYING YES... I would like to start another 'Just Say No' campaign. This one would be on behalf of people who feel the need to say yes to every request of them. This is a campaign for people who put themselves last instead of first.

I plead with all of you to do what is best for humanity and choose to put yourself first. Every single one of us has equal importance. Tend to yourselves as though you were giving to a precious expression of God and then know that you are. From the fullness of yourself you can then tend to others.

Those of us who tend to others first and foremost set limits to our giving, because we begin to fail prematurely. Our health suffers... Our capacity to give wanes...

Maybe 'Just Say Yes' would be a better campaign. Say yes to honoring yourself. Know the truth that you are worthy of nurturing and growth. In our saying yes to ourselves we will create the foundation necessary for all of us to make the choice to Live Beautifully.

> *You can search throughout the entire universe for someone*
> *who is more deserving of your love and affection*
> *than you are yourself,*
> *and that person is not to be found anywhere.*
> *You, yourself,*
> *as much as anybody in the entire universe,*
> *deserve your love and affection.*
> BUDDHA

I INTEND TO SAY YES TO SELF-CARE.

I accept that my days are full... *I relinquish* false beliefs in the scarcity of all that is necessary to care for myself... *I dream of* having the space in my life for self-care... *With peace and love I intend to* honor all of creation including me... *I am grateful* for my daily devotion, *I am.*

*R*EFLECTIONS ON BELONGING... I want to hold your hands and look into the depths of your eyes and speak to you of this truth: "You have nothing to be ashamed of. You are worthy of being accepted just the way you are." I too have lived with shame. I too have lived with the pain of not belonging.

There is no exclusion in this world. Only our perception is flawed. We must adjust our perception and see with new vision. We are worthy of loving and being loved just the way we are.

We must measure our goodness,
not by what we don't do,
what we deny ourselves,
what we resist,
or who we exclude.
Instead we should measure ourselves by what we embrace,
what we create
and who we include.
JACQUES-HENRI BERNARDIN DE SAINT-PIERRE

I INTEND TO LIVE WITH ACCEPTANCE.

I accept that I have believed lies... *I relinquish* judging myself to be unworthy... *I dream of* being aware when my mind is full of icky thinking that pulls me down... *With peace and love I intend to* see the falseness of these thoughts... *I am grateful* to be open to knowing that I belong, *I am.*

When there is silence
one finds the anchor of the universe
within oneself.
LAOZI

*R*EFLECTIONS ON THE SPACE BETWEEN YOUR THOUGHTS… Sit in stillness. Become aware of your breath. Feel the vastness within you. Allow your belly to relax, to soften. Let go of tension.

Feel the energy within you. Breathe into it. Close your eyes. Let it in. Let it out. Step back and observe your breath. Observe the flow. Don't control it. Let it be. Let it flow. Be aware of the stillness. Be aware of the space.

Feel the vibrations. When we are fully aware of the Life within us, we become an exquisitely stringed instrument. Life is so sweet when every string vibrates and resonates, playing a beautiful chord. We are the instrument. Life plays its song through us.

Be Still.
Stillness reveals the secrets of eternity.
LAOZI

I INTEND TO AWAKEN TO THE STILLNESS.

I accept the noisy chatter in my mind… *I relinquish* fears that it will never go away… *I dream of* stillness… *I dream of* peace… *I dream of* sensing the trueness of my being… *With peace and love I intend to* just sit and observe… *I am grateful* for awareness of silence, *I am.*

It is by logic we prove.
It is by intuition we discover.
HENRI POINCARE

𝓡EFLECTIONS ON NAVIGATING… Just as a ship has gauges that are indicators for the captain to determine adjustments that need to be made in order to stay on course for the charted journey, so too do we have gauges that indicate whether we are staying on course. Our body is a fine-tuned machine that gives us feedback if we are willing to listen.

If you feel tension building in your neck, pay attention. You are going off course. Think of it as a red flashing light on a submarine warning its crew of a collision if they don't adjust their course.

What emotion preceded the pain in your neck? What circumstances were you experiencing? Did you bring acceptance to the situation, or were you stressed because you wanted things to be different from what they were? Did anxiety, stress and negativity cut you off from making the choice to Live Beautifully? Did your fearful reaction to a circumstance lead to your discomfort? Pay attention. You are the captain of your vessel. Pay attention to what your gauges are telling you.

Your body will give you the feedback to know when you are going adrift as well as it will tell you when you are smooth sailing. Bon voyage!

We have all a better guide in ourselves,
if we would attend to it,
than any other person can be.
JANE AUSTEN

I INTEND TO BE AWARE OF GUIDANCE.

I accept the aches and pains that sometimes call out to me… *I relinquish* fears of the pain… *I dream of* having the wisdom to listen to the messages… *With peace and love I intend to* be aware of the Guidance that is given… *I am grateful* to choose Upper Realm responses to lower realm situations, *I am.*

REFLECTIONS ON A HEALTHY BODY... Would you like to have a beautiful vibrant body? If a healthy body is what you want, find acceptance and gratitude for all that is. Look reality in the face and accept it. Don't wish for anything to have been different than what it has been. Every circumstance has been perfect for the evolution of your soul. With that acceptance you will come to experience a new kind of existence, an existence that is of a higher frequency.

I believe that our body is a reflection of our thoughts and feelings. A person whose life experience is of angst for what never was, regret for what is, resentment towards others, and pity for oneself will experience a physical self that is a reflection of that energy.

If you live a life of Acceptance, Love and Joy, the physical body that follows will be vibrant and bright. Decide to be less dense. Decide to be a beacon of Light. Practice what you were taught in Sunday school, "This little light of mine, I'm gonna let it shine!"

The greatest revolution in our generation
is the discovery that human beings,
by changing the inner attitudes of their minds,
can change the outer aspects of their lives.
WILLIAM JAMES

I INTEND TO GLOW WITH ACCEPTANCE.

I accept that the physical me reflects the emotional me... *I relinquish* negative thoughts and emotions... *I dream of* being Accepting... *I dream of* being Loving... *I dream of* being Joyful... *With peace and love I intend to* create positive thoughts and emotions... *I am grateful* for my miraculous body, *I am.*

*R*EFLECTIONS ON THOUGHTS... So many of us have desires to live well, to Live Beautifully, but our reality falls short of our ideal. One obstacle that we face in achieving our optimal desires is our own thinking. Our misguided thoughts prevent us from realizing our dreams. We manifest in our lives what we think about. Our thoughts become our reality. This being so, we need to harness the creative energy of our thoughts and focus it as we truly desire. Our focus is key to realizing our dreams.

Take health for example. It is safe to say that we want to live a healthy life. But let's take a look at our thoughts. Are our thoughts of health or of disease? How many of us have joined the Fight Against Breast Cancer? If we understand that we attract what we think about, we will see that if we think about fighting, that is exactly what we will manifest in our lives, a fight against breast cancer.

Let's step back and rethink this. What is it that we really want? Not to fight breast cancer, but to live harmoniously in a healthy body. That being said we need to choose our thoughts accordingly. We need to consciously select our thoughts to only include those of living a healthy life. Do you wish to fight or to live peacefully and lovingly?

Excellence is never an accident.
It is always the result of high intention,
sincere effort, and intelligent execution;
it represents the wise choice of many alternatives –
choice, not chance, determines your destiny.
ARISTOTLE

I INTEND TO LET GO OF NEGATIVE PATTERNS OF THOUGHT.

I accept that thoughts have profound effects... *I relinquish* negative patterns of thought... *I dream of* my mind being healed... *With peace and love I intend to* pay attention to my thinking... *I am grateful* for being Aware, *I am.*

$\mathcal{R}$EFLECTIONS ON SETTING DOWN ROOTS… I've been like a tree growing in a pot that lacked connection to the Earth. I lived with a steady yearning for comfort: to feel content, to feel whole, to feel like I was in the right place. I would seek comfort in a hot cup of coffee or a glass of wine, but these were false substitutes for the comfort that I ached for. And so for a time I went without these pacifiers. Without the substitutes, I endured the pain of breaking free from the pot.

With my contaminated roots exposed, I was bare and vulnerable having to find the courage to open myself up and let go of the past. As the debris is being washed away, I have found myself beginning to set down roots into our Earthly Mother. I am connecting. I am grounding. With my roots grounded to our Earthly Mother and my crown open to the Light of our Heavenly Father, I am beginning to experience the joys of union with Heaven and Earth.

My roots are shallow and I am still plagued with much debris of the past, but I will be patient. With my devotion to healing I will slowly purify and grow strong.

I INTEND TO BE CONNECTED TO HEAVEN AND EARTH.

I accept the discomfort of going without what comforts me to force myself to break free… *I relinquish* habits that pacify my discomfort… *I dream* of setting roots deep into our Earthly Mother… *With peace and love I intend to* release all that blocks my capacity for rootedness… *I am grateful* to be a strong point of Union, *I am.*

All the art of living
lies in a fine mingling
of letting go and holding on.
HENRY ELLIS

REFLECTIONS ON CLEARING THE CLUTTER... For years I read Sarah Ban Breathnach's book, *Simple Abundance*. Each morning it was a joy to sit with my coffee and read her inspirations and write in my journal.

I remember her urges to purge our homes of everything that didn't delight us. If an object didn't bring you joy, she advised you to get rid of it. She urged us to make our homes a beautiful reflection of our authentic selves. And so I followed her advice and room by room I removed the clutter and accumulation of stuff that no longer reflected or served me.

Several years later, I feel like I'm repeating that same process, but on an internal level. I'm stepping back and looking at my thought patterns, my fears, my ways of doing things, my lifestyle, and becoming aware of what brings me joy. If it doesn't bring me joy it goes into the relinquish pile. I am relinquishing fears: fears of not having enough time, fears of not having enough money, fears of not doing the right thing, fears of my children's well-being. I am relinquishing judgment of others and judgment of situations. I am relinquishing repetitive thought. Just as when I hauled out the clutter in my home and created space, there is now space within me. Space for new possibilities.

Whenever there is space creativity has an opportunity to creep in and fill the void. Clear the clutter my friends. Be on high alert for the thoughts and behaviors that bog you down. Cast them aside. Create the space for a new possibility. A life of newfound joy.

When I let go of what I am,
I become what I might be.
LAOZI

I INTEND TO CREATE ORDER AND BEAUTY.

I accept that I accumulate needlessly: stuff, thoughts, fears, behaviors, old emotional pain... *I relinquish* fears of letting go... *I dream of* space, inside and out... *With peace and love I intend to* be aware within... *I am grateful* to be free of false beliefs, negative thinking and old stored pain, *I am.*

Fear is static that prevents me from hearing myself.
SAMUEL BUTLER

*R*EFLECTIONS ON CLEARING THE STATIC... Last night I received very disturbing news about some family friends. My emotions were on high alert. My heart was broken. I was angry. I was confused. I was frustrated. I wanted things to be different. I went to bed feeling very heavy and sad.

This morning the heaviness lingers. My thoughts are stuck on negativity. I feel like it's time to return to stillness, but how?

It reminds me of our television set when I was a little girl. Sometimes it would flicker a line of static across the screen. It might come and go a few times... static, clear picture, static, static, clear picture, static. If it got stuck in static mode, someone would have to get up, walk across the room and give it a good smack. Then it would return to a clear picture. On bad days it would take repeated smacks.

I feel like that old TV stuck in static mode right now. I want to return to clarity, to stillness. I wish someone would come up and whap me upside the head to realign my thought-waves that are all askew.

There's no one to do the job in that regard, so instead I will return to gratitude journaling. I will keep finding Gratitude and reveling in my Appreciation, my Acceptance, and my Joy.

With fits and starts my being slowly returns to clarity. I let go of the negativity, and Acceptance slowly creeps in. My heart regains its joyful vibration once again. Ahhh, it feels so good to return to Lightness and Clarity.

When people will not weed their own minds,
they are apt to be overrun by nettles.
HORACE WALPOLE

I INTEND TO RETURN TO CLARITY.

I accept that I suffer when my thoughts and emotions run wild... *I relinquish* fearful thoughts and emotions as I know they do me harm... *I dream of* the clarity of Love and Light... *With peace and love I intend to* use thoughts of Gratitude as a tool for returning to Clarity... *I am grateful* for awareness of the choice of remaining connected with Love, *I am.*

Everything in excess
is opposed to nature.
HIPPOCRATES

*R*EFLECTIONS ON FRANTIC CONSUMERISM... We seem to have an insatiable hunger for food. We continue to eat even when our body's need for nourishment has long since been met. We want enough. But when we get enough we still want more.

We seem to have an insatiable hunger for stuff as well. When our needs have been met for clothing and shelter, we don't sit down and rest and enjoy. No, we push on for more. More clothing, more shoes, more purses, more furniture, more decorations, and a bigger house to contain it all.

When we are mindful of ourselves we may become aware of desires that keep us in a pattern of satisfying lower realm wantings.

There are few things
we should keenly desire
if we really knew what we wanted.
FRANÇOIS DE LA ROCHEFOUCAULD

I INTEND TO BE MINDFUL OF WANTINGS.

I accept that lower realm circumstances wreak havoc with my life... *I relinquish* judging myself to be less than good enough... *I dream of* feeling content... *With peace and love I intend to* become an observer of my desires... *I am grateful* for the Awareness that allows for me to separate from unhealthy patterns, *I am.*

All differences in this world are of degree,
and not of kind,
because oneness is the secret of everything.
SWAMI VIVEKANANDA

*R*EFLECTIONS ON THE WEB OF LIFE... Before my dear Grandma Lukas passed away she loving entrusted me with some family heirlooms. One of my most cherished is a large tatted doily that was made by Grandpa Lukas' mother. I am astonished at how a woman could start with a spool of thread, a little metal shuttle, and a pattern and end up with an intricate piece of art. I handle the doily with great care as over the years threads have frayed and broken compromising the structure of the overall design.

As I gaze at this doily I am reminded of our universe. One life exquisitely connected by a fine thread. Like my doily, life on this planet is fraying. The physical structure is breaking down. We became blind to our knowledge of the oneness of all and so began our insanity. The insanity that plagues our minds is reflected in our physical world.

Thankfully, I think we have begun to heal. Many people don't just believe that we are one, but have come to sense the truth that All is One. I yearn for humanity to sense that we are a part of a miraculous creation, so that we can live a life of Peace and Joy, instead of pain and isolation. When that wisdom is established, our sanity will return and we will Live Beautifully.

There are often beams in our eye that we know not of.
Let us therefore ask that our eye may become single,
for then we ourselves shall become wholly single.
VINCENT VAN GOGH

I INTEND TO KNOW THAT ALL IS ONE.

I accept that humanity has largely forgotten its Union with All... *I relinquish* fears that I am separate from God... *I dream of* sensing the Oneness of All... *I dream of* having eyes that see with Truth... *With peace and love I intend to* be outdoors as much as possible in a state of Awareness... *I am grateful* that the sense of separation is weakening, *I am.*

Beauty surrounds us.
RUMI

REFLECTIONS ON AN ENCOUNTER WITH ROYALTY... One day I was raking and burning leaves on a gorgeous autumn day. I glanced up and there before me was the most majestic white tail buck I had ever seen. He was a real beauty. He stood before me sniffing the air, my lavender hand lotion and the smoke from the fire blowing directly toward him.

We stood facing each other for quite some time. I was struck by his curiosity and by his beauty. He seemed to pose his large body just like you see on a hunter's magazine cover. He stood in the sunshine with his head turned toward me to show off his splendid 8-point rack.

Although he was physically beautiful, I think what has stayed with me the most was his strong demeanor. He was gentle and yet powerful. He was alert and yet calm.

I too want to be a beautiful creature. I want to embody a splendid mix of energies. I want to be a soft and loving woman and yet a powerful matriarch. I want to be quiet and gentle and yet strong and wise.

Everything has its beauty
but not everyone sees it.
CONFUCIUS

I INTEND TO SEE THE BEAUTY OF THE CREATURES.

I accept that I have judged some qualities to be better than others... *I relinquish* judgment... *I dream of* being true to myself... *With peace and love I intend to* honor diversity... *I am grateful* for awareness of the complex energies of our world, *I am.*

The painter has the Universe in his mind and hands.
LEONARDO DA VINCI

*R*EFLECTIONS ON BOUNTIFUL LIVING... I was recently faced with the possibility of making some significant changes in my lifestyle. I didn't realize just how precious my lifestyle was until I was threatened by the loss of it.

We have been blessed with prosperity for many decades. What have we done with it? Have we used our resources to afford ourselves the luxury of joy? Or have we used our resources to accumulate more and more material possessions?

I think we have squandered our most precious commodity. The time to Be. The time to be Creative. The time to be Joyful. The time to be Loving. I'm ready to change. I want to stop over consuming and instead concentrate my efforts on being with those that I love and doing what I love. I want to Be more than I want to have.

I would highly recommend making a list of all that brings you Joy. After you have completed your list, go back and read it. Slowly, see the unique person that you are. Honor the authentic you by doing what you love. Feel gratitude for the blessing of being an outlet for Love, Joy and Creativity.

The crowning fortune of a man is to be born
to some pursuit which finds him employment and happiness, whether it be to make
baskets,
or broadswords,
or canals,
or statues,
or songs.
RALPH WALDO EMERSON

I INTEND TO BE AUTHENTICALLY ME.

I accept that something special flows into my life when I am doing what I love... *I relinquish* believing that there is a shortage of resources to support the life I dream of... *I dream of* creating the most beautiful life I can possibly imagine... *With peace and love I intend to* express my Divine Life Purpose... *I am grateful* for the joy that comes when I do what I love, *I am.*

What is born will die,
What has been gathered will be dispersed,
What has accumulated will be exhausted,
What has been built up will collapse,
And what has been high will be brought low.
BUDDHA

REFLECTIONS ON THE FLOW... In & out. To & fro. In & out. To & fro. Everywhere I look it's the same. My breath comes in, my breath goes out. My chest rises, my chest falls. Puddles expand, puddles disappear.

In & out. To & fro. In & out. To & fro. The sun rises. The sun sets. The air warms. The air cools. In & out. To & fro. In & out. To & fro. My son grows. My father shrinks.

Ebb & flow. Ebb & flow. The waves roll in. The waves roll out. Expansion. Contraction. Expansion. Contraction.

I live my life ebbing & flowing. My lungs fill, my lungs empty. My stomach fills, my stomach empties. Coming & going. Coming & going. My circle of friends expands. My circle of friends contracts. My house fills. My house empties. We win some. We lose some.

In & out. To & fro. I'm hot. I'm cold. Days turn to night. Darkness turns to Light. The unending Flow of Life.

Life is a series of natural and spontaneous changes.
Don't resist them - that only creates sorrow.
Let reality be reality.
Let things flow naturally forward in whatever way they like.
LAOZI

I INTEND TO EMBRACE THE FLOW OF LIFE.

I accept that life is a continuous ebb and flow... *I relinquish* fears of change... *I dream of* letting go of resistance... *With peace and love I intend to* embrace the flow... *I am grateful* for the ever-changing world that I am a part of, *I am.*

The world is the great gymnasium
where we come to make ourselves strong.
SWAMI VIVEKANANDA

*R*EFLECTIONS ON FEAR... As consciousness begins to expand within me, I feel the grip of fear lessoning. Financial fears, familial fears, fears of abandonment, fears of not being where I am supposed to be: all slowly fading away. There is a density in my abdomen that is lessening as well. I wasn't aware of it until now that I feel it slowly letting go and dispersing.

For so long I was so afraid. I worked so hard to earn more money and to earn the love of those around me, but all of that effort only brought a false sense of confidence. Only through consciousness, awareness of our Oneness, can we truly be Peaceful.

Continue on this journey with me my friends. We're headed in the right direction.

The only journey
is the one within.
RAINER MARIA RILKE

I INTEND TO CHOOSE EACH DAY TO CONTINUE ON MY JOURNEY.

I accept every step of my journey... *I relinquish* fears of scarcity and separation... *I dream of* Healing... *With peace and love I intend to* compassionately embrace Life... *I am grateful* for this beautiful journey, *I am.*

Take up one idea.
Make that one idea your life –
think of it,
dream of it,
live on that idea.
Let the brain,
muscles,
nerves,
every part of your body,
be full of that idea,
and just leave every other idea alone.
This is the way to success.
SWAMI VIVEKANANDA

REFLECTIONS ON CULTIVATION... Seeds of inspiration occur on the expanse of our minds. These seeds are our potential. It is up to us whether these seeds are given the opportunity to grow. We make the choice to say yes to Creation. Offer yourself up. Let your prayer be, "I honor inspiration. I intend it to be. I am willing to birth this creation that I hold within me." Open yourself. Let yourself be an outlet. Enjoy the bliss of being creative.

I dream my painting
and I paint my dream.
VINCENT VAN GOGH

I INTEND TO OPEN MYSELF TO ALLOW LIFE TO COME THROUGH ME.

I accept the possibility of my dreams... *I relinquish* fears of failing... *I dream of* having the courage to try... *With peace and love I intend to* explore my yearnings... *I am grateful* to be open to new possibilities, *I am.*

Don't be too quick to draw conclusions from what happens to you; simply let it happen.
Otherwise it will be too easy for you to look with blame... at your past,
which naturally has a share with everything that now meets you.
RAINER MARIA RILKE

REFLECTIONS ON CLEANING UP YOUR HARD DRIVE... Last week I had just plain old 'had it.' I went for a hike and contemplated letting go of past memories and habitual patterns of behavior. The tension in my back and neck had become acute pain and I could no longer ignore it. I had to let it go.

As I walked I imagined all of my memories and behavioral patterns to be stored within the 'hard drive' of my body. My body felt like a computer that had become bogged down from a lack of maintenance. I needed to delete old useless files and defrag the hard drive. Any memories that I no longer wished to hold on to were transferred to imaginary CDs. I began to eject the CDs from a slot between my shoulder blades. I walked faster and faster as the negative memories fell on the trail behind me. CDs containing the patterns of my unhealthy habits were also ejected from my back.

It was so freeing to let go of it all; to leave it there on the trail. Faster and faster I walked as I lightened my load of all the junk that no longer served me.

The secret of change
is to focus all of your energy,
not on fighting the old,
but on building the new.
SOCRATES

I INTEND TO LET GO OF PAINFUL EMOTIONS AND UNHEALTHY HABITS.

I accept that I have held on to memories and habits that do not serve me... *I relinquish* fears of letting go... *I dream of* being courageous... *With peace and love I intend to* release the past... *I am grateful* to be free of that which bogged me down, *I am.*

REFLECTIONS ON UNWANTED GUESTS... Last night my husband kept 'pushing my buttons' as one might say. But instead of buttons, I imagined him to have been poking the big ugly sleeping ogre that resides within me, a.k.a. the lower realm energies that plague me.

When the ogre is out and about, a shadow is cast on all that surrounds me. Fear and insecurity dominate my being. In the presence of the ogre I was too unaware to recognize what was happening when the ogre then called his monster friend, Mr. Pain Body, and they started to party together.

The party is over and I am feeling exhausted. My emotions have gone wild, my eyes are sore from crying and I'm left with a pounding headache.

The next time that big old ogre and that ugly monster want to trash my peacefulness with their antics, I plan to recognize them for who they are and put an end to their charade.

I INTEND TO BECOME AWARE OF MY TRIGGERS.

I accept that there are triggers that stir darkness within me... *I relinquish* fears of this pattern never ending... *I dream of* having Awareness... *With peace and love I intend to* remain on high alert for my reaction to the triggers... *I am grateful* to be waking up, *I am.*

Don't tell me the moon is shining;
show me the glint of light on broken glass.
ANTON CHEKOV

*R*EFLECTIONS ON THE ANTIDOTE FOR PAIN... When we find ourselves in a tail spin and we are faced with agonizing pain, both physical or emotional, what do we do? How do we stop the insanity?

I find it beneficial to pull myself back up by focusing on inspirational quotes, prayers and writings. I crowd out the fearful thinking by focusing on reading Truth. And from that place, a moment of stillness may come.

From that place, I can breathe. Just breathe. I can find a corner of solitude and sit. I can feel the anxiety within my body. I can become aware of the swirling of thoughts and emotions. I can acknowledge what is.

Then I can make the choice to simply focus on my breath. My thoughts may come back. I'll return to my breath. My heart may pound. I'll return to my breath. My stomach may turn. I'll come back to my breath. I'll just be aware of my breath.

With practice, I may be able to feel a bout of anxiety coming on and by merely becoming aware of my breath, I may prevent the fearful thoughts and emotions from snowballing into a full blown panic attack. When I am aware of my breath or reading inspired works, it takes my attention away from fueling the darkness that attempts to feed on my thoughts, my emotions and anyone else that it can draw in.

Drag your thoughts away from your troubles...
by the ears, by the heels,
or any other way you can manage it.
MARK TWAIN

I INTEND TO BE PREPARED WITH TOOLS TO REDIRECT MY MIND.

I accept that the old residual pain that I carry creates fearful thinking that attempts to disconnect me from Awareness... *I relinquish* the false beliefs that result in the fearful emotions that create the fearful repetitive thinking... *I dream of* stillness... *With peace and love I intend to* practice breath Awareness or focus on inspired text in moments when the darkness seeks to feed itself... *I am grateful* to be weakening the parasites within me with Awareness, *I am.*

For every minute you remain angry, you give up sixty seconds of peace of mind.
RALPH WALDO EMERSON

*R*EFLECTIONS ON A LESSON TAUGHT... I would like to become a better student in this classroom called Life. It seems that each lesson is just another opportunity to choose Love and Forgiveness. If we fail to choose Love and Forgiveness, Life creates a whole set of new circumstances to give us another chance at learning the lesson at hand. Each time that we fail to choose Love, the pain seems to intensify. Life is a very patient teacher. Many lessons seem to be taking generations to learn.

In my efforts of being a better student, I will begin the practice of reflecting on my experiences and taking note of life's lessons that seem to be on my agenda. I will recall the times when I chose to be angry, agitated, tense or any other lower realm state of being.

Then I will imagine how the situation would have felt different if instead of being drawn into the drama of it all, if I had found Peace and Acceptance for what was. It will be a role play in my imagination. Instead of anger or regret adding negative energy to the environment, I could at the very least remain neutral.

Beyond Acceptance, I could then imagine myself feeling Love and Compassion for those involved. I could take a few moments to pray for humanity that we might find Peace within ourselves and thus with each other. My Love and Compassion would contribute a flow of positive energy into our world.

Negative, neutral, or positive (fearful, Accepting, or Loving), over and over again we get to choose what contribution we will make. For every minute we remain unloving, we give up sixty seconds of Living Beautifully.

When anger rises, think of the consequences.
CONFUCIUS

I INTEND TO CONTRIBUTE LOVE.

I accept that I have responded to what I feel powerless to change with anxiety, resentment, worry, anger and tension... *I relinquish* responding to fear with more of the same... *I dream of* having a spirit that has strength and stamina... *With peace and love I intend to* respond to lower realm situations with an Upper Realm response of Love, Kindness, Compassion or Awareness... *I am grateful* to respond to darkness with Light, *I am... I am grateful* to have a healing presence, *I am.*

~ 48 ~

*R*EFLECTIONS ON BECOMING THE SILENT WATCHER... If you wanted to learn to cook, how might you go about learning to do so? Would you read a cookbook cover to cover trying your best to intellectually absorb all of the techniques? After reading one cookbook would you read yet another? Would you accumulate a wealth of knowledge before you decided to step foot into the kitchen and give it a try?

Of course not, but that seems to be what many of us spiritual seekers are doing. We buy one book after another, and read and read thinking that our understanding will lead us closer to spiritual enlightenment. At some point we have to tell ourselves that it is time to put down the books and 'step into the kitchen.' All of the reading and thinking doesn't lead to spiritual enlightenment any more than reading a cookbook will lead to a cake on the countertop.

So you've closed the book, now where do you start? Begin by learning to observe your mind. Just observe your thoughts. Observe your emotions. Observe your body. Don't think, don't do, just be, just be an observer. Become aware. You may get distracted and get wrapped up in the goings-on in your mind, but keep coming back to Awareness. Keep returning to being the observer.

If, then, I were asked for the most important advice I could give,
that which I considered to be the most useful to the men of our century,
I should simply say:
in the name of God, stop a moment, cease your work, look around you.
LEO TOLSTOY

I INTEND TO BE AWARE.

I accept my restless mind... *I relinquish* judging my thoughts... *I dream of* having Awareness... *With peace and love I intend to* commit to caring for myself by meditating... *I am grateful* for peaceful moments, *I am.*

In natural science
the principles of truth ought to be confirmed by observation.
Carl Linnaeus

𝓡EFLECTIONS ON BECOMING AWARE OF THE VEIL… Did you ever learn something new, like of a place that you had never heard of before, and then you find yourself suddenly aware that people have been talking of the place all along, but it must have just gone right over your head? And you think, "How could I have missed this all along?"

So it is with the veil that obscures my awareness of the Truth. I am becoming aware of this illusion when I see the stream of repetitive thoughts running through my head: the pain of my past and my fears of the future. I am often so consumed by fearful thoughts that I have little capacity to enjoy life right now. I am beginning to be aware of this not only in myself, but in others as well. How could I have felt so alone in my suffering? How could I have been so consumed by the grip of the lower realm that I didn't see my neighbor in the same predicament?

In moments of Awareness we can observe ourselves with Compassion. We can see that which obscures our knowledge of the Truth as a nasty black plague infecting our beautiful being. The voice we hear that speaks of guilt, scarcity, unworthiness and regret is not Truth. It is the result of old dark energies that plague us. It is our belief in these thoughts that creates the illusion that we are separate from God. When we mistake that voice for our Truth, a veil falls over our eyes and we cease to know our Oneness with All. Then instead of enjoying the blessing of creating our lives with Love, we fall under illusion and strive to control our lives out of fear. Fears that all stem from our false sense of separation from the Whole. I choose to become an observer. I choose to stand still. I choose to be Aware.

There is an old illusion. It is called good and evil.
Friedrich Nietzsche

I INTEND TO BE AWARE OF MY MIND.

I accept the falseness of the mental chatter… *I relinquish* belief in thoughts of doubt… *I dream of* being aware of lower realm thoughts, inspired thoughts and functional thoughts… *With peace and love I intend to* be aware of whether I am creating with Love or controlling out of fear… *I am grateful* that a flicker of Light has been turned on in me, *I am.*

We can easily forgive a child who is afraid of the dark;
the real tragedy of life is when men are afraid of the light.
PLATO

*R*EFLECTIONS ON GOTHAM CITY... Last night on a long drive home from Louisiana, my family watched *Batman Begins* as I drove. I couldn't see the picture, but I listened to the dialogue and the music.

In the movie Wayne fights the evils that plague Gotham City. It struck me as darkness fighting darkness. If he really wanted to end the darkness of corruption in Gotham City, why did he add more darkness to the metropolis? More darkness, more fear, more violence...

It reminded me of my desires for my own little metropolis to be free of corruption, free of that voice in our heads that speaks incessantly of doubt and fear. When the darkness that plagues us is hungry for the lower realm circumstances that feed it, how do we respond? Wayne style? Do we react with an attitude of, "I can't believe that I have to put up with this! I'm sick and tired of it!" (More unacceptance, more victimization, more darkness.) Or do we accept the situation for what it is and express Love and Compassion for the person who is painfully in the grip of what plagues them? Add darkness or add Light? Based on my color-mixing skills of elementary school, I do believe that the addition of Light is going to be our best choice to achieve our desired outcome.

When faced with darkness, shine your Light of Awareness on it. Move over Batman, you've had your chance to defeat the evils of Gotham City. Now it is our turn. Instead of arming ourselves with weapons for fighting evil, we will dissipate the darkness with the Light of our Awareness!

There never was a good war or a bad peace.
BENJAMIN FRANKLIN

I INTEND TO CREATE PEACE.

I accept the darkness that plagues us... *I relinquish* fears of it... *I dream of* being Aware of darkness... *With peace and love I intend to* respond to darkness with Light... *I am grateful* for Healing, *I am.*

For each new morning with its light,
For rest and shelter of the night,
For health and food,
For love and friends,
For everything Thy goodness sends.
RALPH WALDO EMERSON

REFLECTIONS ON A HOLIDAY PASSED... Another holiday has come and gone. All of the groceries have come and the last of the leftovers are gone. The family has come and the family has gone. And so too has the pain in my back, it has come and it has gone.

I have come to realize that I can pretty much bet that I will have a backache when I host a holiday gathering. All of my negative thoughts become fearful emotions, which become tension in my lower back. I fear the magnitude of shopping, food preparation and the cleaning of the house. I fear relatives who may drink excessively and those who may challenge my opinions.

This year I was able to separate myself from the pain. I had an "Ah, there it is again" awareness.

My body is a reflection of my thoughts and feelings. I will keep choosing thoughts of Acceptance, Love and Joy and I will experience a vibrant body. When I slip into thoughts of fear my body will serve as a reminder of the error in my ways. Hopefully I will respond to the twinges. But sometimes I manage to ignore the subtle symptoms and a full-blown pain attack is necessary to stop me in my tracks.

He who has overcome his fears
will truly be free.
ARISTOTLE

I INTEND TO NOTICE FEAR REFLECTED IN OUR BODIES.

I accept that I have fearful thought patterns... *I relinquish* the old habits that do not serve me... *I dream of* having awareness of my body's messages... *With peace and love I intend to* create a beautiful life... *I am grateful* to begin anew, *I am.*

*R*EFLECTIONS ON THE VESSEL I ABIDE IN... Today during Tai Chi class I experienced a deep level of appreciation and love for my body. I'm not talking about some kind of egotistical love, no "Oh my, look how gorgeous I am." Instead I realized how miraculous my body is. I felt gratitude for its fortitude. Despite the lack of high quality food I often give it, it makes do and keeps regenerating itself. Despite my out-of-control emotions, it manages the impact of the stress and keeps going. Despite an incredibly rapidly changing world, it keeps adapting.

This experience has left me with reverence and respect. It leaves me with the yearning to care for my body. I intend to feed myself well. I intend to give myself the rest I need. I intend for my body to be a peaceful healthy reflection of a cheerful loving me.

I intend to move my body in exercise that is beneficial. I don't want to 'put it through the ringer' anymore.

Respect was invented
to cover the empty place
where love should be.
LEO TOLSTOY

I INTEND TO HONOR MYSELF WITH KINDNESS.

I accept how I have treated myself... *I relinquish* judging my body... *I dream of* being aware of the affects of judging my body... *With peace and love I intend to* be Kind... *I am grateful* for my physical resilience, *I am.*

External nature is only internal nature writ large.
SWAMI VIVEKANANDA

*R*EFLECTIONS ON THE SKIN YOU'RE IN... When our daughter was in the 8th grade she was ready to begin expressing herself through her clothing. Previously she had been very happy to wear blue jeans and an athletic t-shirt. We went school shopping and she soon had a typical 13-year-old wardrobe full of the latest fashions. By the spring of that same school year I encountered her in our bedroom hallway toting a large laundry basket of clothing. She confidently told me that we should give these clothes away as they no longer suited her. That was followed up by a request to go shopping because she desperately needed something to wear.

The financially responsible side of me noted that it was foolish to go out and replace clothing that was perfectly fine. But the maternal side of me knew that our daughter was making a transition; she was discovering her authentic self and the clothing that we had purchased did not suit the emerging young girl. She wanted her exterior to be a reflection of her true inner self.

And now many years later, I find myself at a similar crossroads. Many of the clothes in my closet no longer appeal to me. I stand in front of all those clothes and feel like I don't have a thing to wear. I've changed.

I've transformed on the inside. I, too, want my outer expression to reflect the inner me. Just as a fawn loses its spots, a bird goes through a molt, or a caterpillar grows wings, I too am ready to let the physical me reflect the inner me.

*A poor original
is better than a good imitation.*
ELLA WHEELER WILCOX

I INTEND TO EXPRESS MYSELF AUTHENTICALLY.

I accept that I am evolving... *I relinquish* fears of the changes... *I dream of* being at peace expressing the authentic me... *With peace and love I intend to* make my outer beauty a reflection of my inner beauty... *I am grateful* for the freedom to be uniquely me, *I am.*

EFLECTIONS ON THE GREAT PRETENDER... I feel like playing dress up today. I would like to transform myself into something more, like a little girl adorning herself with a long strand of pearls, a feather-plumed hat, and mom's high heels. I want to stand in front of a big trunk filled with possibilities for transforming me into the beautiful woman I long to be.

Instead of my trunk being filled with boas, hats and dresses, I imagine it to be filled with all of the qualities that I admire in a beautiful woman. My trunk holds many possibilities for me to try on: graciousness, self-confidence, strength and compassion. In my dress-up game I can transform myself into the woman I long to be. As I adorn myself with the qualities I long to possess, I feel myself being weighed down with more. There has been an error in my way.

There in the corner I spot yet another trunk. I peer into it to discover more possibilities. But I find that it is empty. I realize that this is the trunk that holds the true opportunity for me to become the beautiful woman I long to be. For I already am that woman. God created me so. What I need to do is remove the superficial layers to reveal the true me. Into this trunk I will cast the garb that obscures the real me: fear, self-doubt, judgment, and arrogance....

Instead of a game of dress up to become the beautiful woman I long to be, I've indulged myself in a game of casting off to reveal the beautiful woman that I am. Into this trunk go all of the beliefs in the lower realm thoughts. On goes the large lock and I shove the trunk to the dark recesses of the basement to be forgotten. I have discovered myself to be the woman of my dreams. She was there all the while, a perfect creation of Light and Love. Welcome home sunshine.

Beauty of style, harmony, grace and good rhythm depend on simplicity...
PLATO

I INTEND TO CAST OFF THAT WHICH OBSCURES THE BEAUTIFUL ME.

I accept myself exactly as I am… *I relinquish* fears of unworthiness... *I relinquish* judgment of myself... *I dream of* letting go of the need to appear as anything other than the authentic me... *With peace and love I intend to* honor my perfection... *I am grateful* to discard that which has obscured the real me, *I am.*

Nothing is at last sacred
but the integrity of your own mind.
RALPH WALDO EMERSON

*R*EFLECTIONS ON "WHO'S IN CHARGE HERE ANYWAY?"... My mind has developed a mind of its own. It has chattered away relentlessly. Sometimes I just want to scream, "Shut up!" so I can get a little peace and quiet. Even in the wee hours of the night I can wake up and not be able to get back to sleep because my mind is going a million miles an hour fretting over this and that.

I've had it. Who's in charge here anyway? Things are going to change. From now on my brain will be my tool. When I need it I will use it. And when I'm done I'm hitting the off button. No more swirling of useless worrisome thoughts. When my brain stays on for all of that useless thought it drains me of energy. It leaves me worn out and frazzled.

Who's in charge here? I'm in charge!!!

Silence is a source of Great Strength.
LAOZI

I INTEND TO ENJOY THE BLISS OF SILENCE WITHIN.

I accept that my mind needs healing... *I relinquish* the fears and doubts that plague my being... *I dream of* Healing... *I dream of* Awareness... *I dream of* Stillness... *I dream of* Peace... *I dream of* Serenity... *With peace and love I intend to* be Tranquil... *I am grateful* for awareness of the falseness of crazy thinking, *I am.*

A little insomnia is not without its value
in making us appreciate sleep,
in throwing a ray of light
upon that darkness.
MARCEL PROUST

*R*EFLECTIONS ON A PEACEFUL SLUMBER... A day spent living with a frantic mind leads to a night spent in a body that is tense with aches and pains and a brain that just won't stop. Our inability to turn off the senseless activities of the mind leads to fatigue by day and sleeplessness by night.

Choose to Live Beautifully. Keep returning to stillness by day. Not a stillness in the sense of inactivity, but a Peaceful Stillness within. Expand your awareness of the Stillness by turning your awareness to your Breath for a few moments over and over throughout the day.

A ruffled mind
makes a restless pillow.
CHARLOTTE BRONTE

I INTEND TO BE AWARE OF THE BREATH.

I accept that my restless mind is the source of my agony... *I relinquish* fears and judgments... *I dream of* Healing... *I dream of* being an astute observer of my mind so that I can recognize when the useless thought is present... *I dream of* knowing that I am not alone in my suffering... *With peace and love I intend to* return to Awareness of my Breath... *I am grateful* for every step on my journey that is leading to Peace, *I am.*

Where there is charity and wisdom,
there is neither fear nor ignorance.
Where there is patience and humility,
there is neither anger nor vexation.
Where there is poverty and joy,
there is neither greed nor avarice.
Where there is peace and meditation,
there is neither anxiety nor doubt.
ST. FRANCIS OF ASSISI

*R*EFLECTIONS ON A RESOLUTION… It's time for me to make a resolution. My resolution: to build strength and stamina to get me through the challenging times. I won't be working out at the gym though. The strength I speak of is spiritual strength. Spiritual stamina.

The last month brought on a hustle and bustle of activities. Soon I found it difficult to turn off the lower realm thinking that plagued my being. It was back. Sometimes you don't realize how precious something is until you don't have it anymore. My Peaceful Presence was fragmented at best. The darkness had once again taken over my mind and fear returned to my being.

I want to develop the spiritual stamina to stay present not just in quiet moments of solitude, but in the midst of activity and turmoil. My morning meditation and reflection will be a daily workout regime for my spirit.

Work is not always required.
There is such a thing as sacred idleness.
GEORGE MACDONALD

I INTEND TO COMMIT TO A DAILY MORNING MEDITATION.

I accept the comings and goings of Peacefulness… *I relinquish* believing the fears and judgments that plague my mind… *I dream of* having the space in my life to sit in Stillness, Prayer and Reflection at the start of each and every day… *With peace and love I intend to* honor this part of my life with devotion… *I am grateful* for my daily meditation, *I am.*

REFLECTIONS ON DREAMING OF LIVING BEAUTIFULLY... Let's go on a trip; a journey of our imaginations. Take an hour or so to let your mind wander. Your destination is an imaginary world where you are Living Beautifully exactly as you uniquely define it. Don't hold back. Let your imagination soar. Deny fear. Our yearnings are the nudges of seeds that are trying to sprout from within us. Once you've developed the mental image, revel in actually living your life in your wonderland. Anything is possible. Just dream. Dream of Living Beautifully exactly as you uniquely define it.

I INTEND TO DARE TO DREAM BIG.

I accept that there are gifts for me to bring forth... *I relinquish* fears of dreaming too much... *I dream of* having the faith to believe in the worthiness of my desires... *With peace and love I intend to* honor my Yearnings... *I am grateful* for awareness of the potential within me, *I am.*

Whatever you do, you need courage.
Whatever course you decide upon,
there is always someone to tell you that you are wrong.
There are always difficulties arising that tempt you
to believe your critics are right.
To map out a course of action and follow it to an end
requires some of the same courage that a soldier needs.
Peace has its victories,
but it takes brave men and women to win them.
RALPH WALDO EMERSON

*R*EFLECTIONS ON BEGINNING YOUR JOURNEY... We've indulged ourselves in a daydream, an imaginary journey into living our authentic lives. Today I invite you to take one step in the direction of that dream. You don't have to jump right in. Just dip your toe into the pool. Explore indulging yourself into taking one small step. All journeys are taken one small step at a time. Muster up the courage to respond to your Yearnings.

To accomplish great things,
we must dream as well as act.
ANATOLE FRANCE

I INTEND TO SAY YES TO THE NUDGES.

I accept my nervousness as I consider the possibility of my dreams... *I relinquish* fears of anyone seeing me fail... *I dream of* sensing the Nudges... *With peace and love I intend to* honor Inspiration as Creation attempting to come forth into our world... *I am grateful* to be Inspired, *I am.*

The eye by which I see God
is the same eye by which God sees me.
MEISTER ECKHART

*R*EFLECTIONS ON THE TRUTH WITHIN... Meditation is like a cleaning of the slate. As I quiet myself and settle in, my mind is still active. I compassionately dismiss the thoughts that arise. At first there are many but slowly my mind surrenders and quiets itself.

Once my mind is at rest the Bliss begins. I can be in my body at Peace. I can sense the aliveness. I can feel the movement of energies. In the Stillness I am energized. I have sensed who I am.

My lifetime of searching for answers has been to no avail, my Truth was within myself all the while. Instead of action, I needed to still myself. The treasure I was seeking wasn't in a far off land, it wasn't in an achievement or acquisition. The treasure I sought was Peace. It was right here all the time. The treasure I searched for was within.

We may explore the universe and find ourselves,
or we may explore ourselves and find the universe.
It matters not which of these paths we choose.
DIANA GARDNER ROBINSON

I INTEND TO BE AWARE WITHIN.

I accept the reality of mankind... *I relinquish* fear, anger, judgment, shame, unworthiness... *I dream of* living a life of Peace... *With peace and love I intend to* live with Kindness... *I am grateful* to be Aware, *I am.*

The real voyage of discovery
consists not in seeking new landscapes,
but in having new eyes.
MARCEL PROUST

*R*EFLECTIONS ON SPRING CLEANING… I'm going to begin a new slant in my gratitude journaling. I am going to express gratitude for Life. Not just the parts that I have perceived to be good, but all of it. In looking back I will know that all of my life experiences have been neither good nor bad. Life has given me the perfect circumstances for the evolution of my soul. I will accept them. I will feel gratitude for all that is. I will choose to be nourished by the memories of all that felt good and I will choose to let go of the negativity from resisting anything that I perceived to be bad.

It will be a cleaning out of my closet so to speak. All skeletons of the past are going to have to find a new place to reside because I'm doing a major spring cleaning job of anything in my lifetime that doesn't fit the new me. The new me is optimistic and sunny no matter if I am looking forward to my future or back at my past.

I'm going to be sporting a new mental outlook this season. It will be a fresh new look. One of Acceptance, Peace and Joy. Please join me in cleaning out your own closet.

To progress
is always to begin again.
MARTIN LUTHER

I INTEND TO JOYFULLY ACCEPT LIFE.

I accept every moment of my life… *I relinquish* judgment of moments… *I dream of* having new eyes… *With peace and love I intend to* live with a joyful heart… *I am grateful* for Life, *I am.*

We join spokes together in a wheel,
but it is the center hole that makes the wagon move.
We shape clay into a pot,
but it is the emptiness inside that holds whatever we desire.
We hammer wood for a house,
but it is the inner space that makes it livable.
We work with being,
but nonbeing is what we use.
LAOZI

REFLECTIONS ON STILLNESS... We focus on being: being Forgiving, being Accepting, being Joyful. For being is necessary for our ultimate outcome of nonbeing, Stillness.

Being is the spoke that creates the center hole. Being is the clay that creates the space within the pot. Being is the structure that creates the space within.

Being is necessary, but not the end. Just be, and at the center of being, find Stillness.

I am a hole in a flute
that the Christ's breath moves through.
Listen to the music.
HAFIZ

I INTEND TO RETURN TO STILLNESS.

I accept when I am restless... *I relinquish* judgment of myself... *I dream of* having Awareness of the Stillness within... *With peace and love I intend to* just be... *I am grateful* for the Joy that fills my heart, *I am.*

*R*EFLECTIONS ON JUDGING... Sometimes I am judgmental of others and the things that they do. I watch them and shake my head. It strengthens false beliefs in superiority when I believe myself to be better than someone else.

Other times I judge myself. I look in the mirror and judge my appearance over and over again.

The next time I see a fellow human being struggling, instead of judgment I will choose Awareness. I will see souls who yearn to break free of what binds them to the lower realm so that they can spread their wings and fly.

Judgment fuels the lower realm circumstances. Awareness is a Light that illuminates the darkness of the lower realm. I yearn to be Compassionate towards our human race as we struggle to fully emerge and fly in the Upper Realms of existence.

I INTEND TO LIVE WITH COMPASSION.

I accept that I have felt justified in judging lower realm experiences... *I relinquish* the tendency to respond with defensiveness when I feel the discomfort of lower realm energies... *I dream of* sensing low energies and responding with acute Awareness... *With peace and love I intend to* follow up a lower realm interaction with a reflective time to seek Awareness of myself and other peoples' errors of acting on lower realm beliefs... *I am grateful* for the healing affects of the Light of Awareness, *I am.*

I have always found
that mercy bears richer results
than strict justice.
ABRAHAM LINCOLN

REFLECTIONS ON STRENGTHENING MY SPIRIT... Something special happens as we practice forgiveness. When we forgive something leaves us. There is a letting go. In the moment of true forgiveness something else enters us and replaces the old negativity. Our fears leave and we become infused with a dose of Divine energy, Grace.

Each little act of forgiveness causes a change in our Self, in the energy that makes up our being. As we let go of our fears and practice forgiveness the negativity that manifested as tension in our jaws or pains in our backs gets released.

As Divine energy flows in, our bodies become more vibrant. Pain and tension fall away. Rigidity comes when you wish for something different than what is or what was. Flexibility comes when you accept what is... forgive the past... and see it all with compassionate loving eyes.

The world is a looking glass
and gives back to every man the reflection of his own face.
WILLIAM MAKEPEACE THACKERAY

I INTEND TO BE FORGIVING.

I accept that I have held onto resentment for the past... *I relinquish* judgment of the circumstances and the people involved... *I dream of* having eyes that see with Love... *With peace and love I intend to* be Compassionate and Kind... *I am grateful* to live in this moment unencumbered by thoughts of judgment of the past, *I am.*

Dwell on the beauty of life.
Watch the stars, and see yourself running with them.
MARCUS AURELIUS

*R*EFLECTIONS ON BEING RENDERED SPEECHLESS… Some moments in my life have been too big for words. Occasionally I have been blessed by moments that have rendered me speechless and sometimes have even taken my breath away: the beauty of a sunset, a window intricately covered with frost, the sight of my child in a peaceful slumber. Mere thoughts and words cannot begin to touch the experience of these moments. These moments are experienced as pure Joy.

Beauty. Love. Joy. None of these come to me through thought. I experience them with my being. I yearn to turn off the obsessive voice in my head so that I might be more inclined to experience rapturous moments of Joy.

The turning off of the voice in my head is a slow steady transformation. One path I know is to be conscious of my Breath. I have little acorns scattered about my home. I carry them in my pocket, my purse, in my car… They are little reminders to turn my Awareness to my breath for a moment. They are little reminders to turn my focus toward that which turns acorns into oaks.

Those who seek the truth by means of the intellect and learning
only get further and further away from it.
Not till your thoughts cease all their branching here and there,
not till you abandon all thoughts of seeking for something,
not till your mind is motionless as wood or stone,
will you be on the right road to the Gate.
HUANG PO

I INTEND TO BE AWARE.

I accept that Joy has never come to me through thinking… *I relinquish* trying to find Joy through finding the right answers… *I dream of* sensing Guidance that will nudge me back throughout my day to moments of Awareness… *With peace and love I intend to* use the acorn as a reminder to return to Awareness of my Breath… *I am grateful* for Awareness of the Life Force within me that turns acorns into oaks, *I am.*

To err is human, to forgive, divine.
ALEXANDER POPE

*R*EFLECTIONS ON SETTING DOWN YOUR BAGGAGE… I had a wonderful morning today. I set off on my bike ride feeling on top of the world. As I rode down a path I approached a woman running alongside a little girl on a bike. They didn't hear my approach so with just a few yards separating us I let out a friendly "Good Morning!" I was surprised by the woman's reaction. She let out a scream and threw her arms in the air. She came to a dead stop and bent at the waist to recover from her explosion of emotion. When she straightened herself, she looked at me and said, "I feel like I just lost five pounds." Thinking that losing five pounds is every woman's dream come true, I replied, "You're welcome," and continued to ride past them.

As I peddled along I contemplated what I had just witnessed. The phrase that came to mind was, "I scared the begeebies out of her." I felt as though I literally witnessed a release of old negative energies. Like the energy literally let loose from her body, thus the flailing of arms, the screams and the subsequent sensation of her body feeling five pounds lighter.

Many of us carry the emotional baggage of our past within us. It's like we have a pack on our backs and we keep adding to our load. Why do we carry the negative energies of the past? Do old painful energies create the stinkin' thinkin' in order to sustain itself? Does this old pain continue to survive on the emotions that we generate from believing and acting on these fearful thoughts? Do we keep feeding these old energies the negative energy of our fearful emotions? Would it be wise to see this situation with awareness and pray for healing of our minds? Thus we would be free to forgive, forget and move on?

An eye for an eye, and the whole world would be blind.
KAHLIL GIBRAN

I INTEND TO BE AWARE OF THE DARK ENERGIES THAT PLAGUE ME.

I accept that I carry lower realm energies… *I relinquish* the chains that bind me to the past… *I dream of* freedom from pain… *With peace and love I intend to* receive the healing of my mind, my body and my spirit… *I am grateful* for forgiveness, *I am.*

*R*EFLECTIONS ON SELF-CARE... As I dutifully perform the supportive tasks for my children and husband I sometimes hear a whisper. It says to me, "I have a plan for you too Doris."

I've been caught up in playing the supportive role of wife and mother for so long that I don't give much effort to bringing my other gifts into this world. I was taught that it is better to give than to receive. But give what? Solely give of my efforts to support my loved ones' gifts? Or give of my own gifts as well?

I recently went to the movie theatre. I was frustrated by how many movies were based on fear and violence. Where were the movies that I wished to see? Were they held in the hearts of people who out of guilt tend to other's gifts instead of their own?

Join me as we acknowledge our gifts. Know that deep within you there is a seed that yearns to be given the opportunity to bloom. Stand up and volunteer to be the vessel that brings forth this Creation. Let's open ourselves to give birth, to be fertile ground for a glorious Creation.

What you can do,
or dream you can—
begin it.
Boldness has genius,
power and magic in it.
JOHANN WOLFGANG GOETHE

I INTEND TO BIRTH THE CREATION THAT IS WITHIN ME.

I accept that I too have a worthy gift to share with our world... *I relinquish* fears of trying and of failing... *I relinquish* needing to know how it will happen... *I dream of* having the strength to believe in myself and the knowing that it will all work out... *With peace and love I intend to* honor the Inspirations by expressing them... *I am grateful* for awareness of the Potential that is within me, *I am.*

Destiny is not a matter of chance;
it is a matter of choice.
It is not a thing to be waited for;
it is a thing to be achieved.
WILLIAM JENNINGS BRYAN

*R*EFLECTIONS ON WHAT IS POSSIBLE… Traveling on a remote country road today, I saw an old red barn. The owners had posted a message on its side in huge letters. It read, "Anything is possible, with love."

My destination was the Kettle Moraine State Park. As I hiked along a scenic trail enjoying the splendor of autumn's beauty, I contemplated the barn owner's motivation and their message. They must have felt that this message had great significance to justify their efforts and expenditures.

So what does this message mean to me? I think we are tired of being the victims of this or that. I think we want to choose to express our own will. I think we want to make choices for ourselves, not follow the advice of others out of fear. I believe that our reclaiming our freedom of choice, made strong by a foundation of Love, will result in greatness.

Let the beauty of what you love
be what you do.
RUMI

I INTEND TO CHOOSE TO CREATE WITH LOVE.

I accept that out of fear I have tried to control… *I relinquish* living in darkness… *I dream of* knowing that "Anything is possible, with love…" *With peace and love I intend to* be aware of when I have sought control from a place of victimization… *I am grateful* to Create with Love, *I am.*

The energy of the mind is the essence of life.
ARISTOTLE

*R*EFLECTIONS ON RETURNING TO STILLNESS... I experienced the most enjoyable afternoon; so full of Awareness and Creativity. It was like I had arrived at a splendid state of Consciousness. Or so I thought I had arrived to stay for an eternity. But much to my surprise a few short hours later I would find myself in a difficult situation that twisted my emotions around and around so tight that returning to stillness required a realignment of major magnitude.

I was like a pit bull with a vengeance. My mind didn't want to let go of the unjustness of the entire situation. It was held tightly in my jaws and I was drooling and shaking my head from side to side. I recognized my insanity. But what do you do to return to that blissful state of being?

Breathe, breathe, breathe, slower, breathe deeper, find stillness within, listen, let it go, shake it off, choose, let the negativity of this moment become a part of my energy or let it go, let it end, make a choice, carry the load or put it down. Put it down, don't fuel it, and let it return to nothingness. It expanded, it grew, I fueled it, now I will let it go, pay it no bother, without my attention, my energy, it will fade away. It will contract until it is no more.

In its place Consciousness will expand. The Stillness will expand. I can return Home once again.

It is in your power to withdraw yourself whenever you desire.
Perfect tranquility within consists in the good ordering of the mind,
the realm of your own.
MARCUS AURELIUS

I INTEND TO FOCUS MY ATTENTION WILLFULLY.

I accept that craziness sometimes creeps in... *I relinquish* fears of moments of insanity... *I dream of* having Awareness of my thinking... *With peace and love I intend to* be gentle with myself as I go through this transition... *I am grateful* for awareness of the choice I have to hold on or to let go, *I am.*

You do not need to leave your room…
Remain sitting at your table and listen.
Do not even listen, simply wait.
Do not even wait, be quite still and solitary.
The world will freely offer itself to you to be unmasked.
It has no choice.
It will roll in ecstasy at your feet.
FRANZ KAFKA

REFLECTIONS ON NOURISHING MY SOUL… The voice in my head is relentless. It is a force to be reckoned with over and over again. And it seems to rear its ugly head at the most inopportune times. When life brings chaos, the ick seems to jump right in when I'm distracted. I yearn to maintain Awareness. Indulging myself in a morning meditation seems to be my best defense against darkness.

I think of meditation as a sort of 'plugging in.' I need to regularly 'plug in my Light of Awareness' to maintain my charge. Without it my battery seems to fade. I need to keep returning over and over again to get my Light recharged. Morning is a great time for me to meditate. I find it easier to quiet my mind as the day hasn't yet filled my head with distractions.

Just as I nourish my physical body over and over again, I must feed myself with meditation over and over again. Both meditations in a chair as well as meditative walks in nature restore myself to health. I will honor my soul's need for daily nourishment right along with my body's need for nourishment.

Some keep the Sabbath going to Church,
I keep it staying at Home -
With a bobolink for a Chorister,
And an Orchard, for a Dome.
EMILY DICKINSON

I INTEND TO NOURISH MYSELF: MIND, BODY AND SPIRIT.

I accept that I need daily nourishment… *I relinquish* fears of not having enough time… *I dream of* having the wisdom to nourish myself wisely… *With peace and love I intend to* commit to connecting with a daily meditation…. *I am grateful* for the Grace that flows into me, *I am.*

Or, rather, let us be more simple and less vain.
JEAN-JACQUES ROUSSEAU

℟EFLECTIONS ON THE GRAND ILLUSION... Lately I've been meeting new people socially. As soon as we get beyond exchanging our handshakes, our names, and our home-towns, I feel like the ego jumps out from behind a bush and says, "Don't forget about me! Me, me, me... introduce me!" And I find myself sharing my titles, my roles, my identities, all for the purpose of enhancing the egoic me. It's like a collection of lower realm beliefs get mutually reinforced in those first moments.

Have you ever watched children at play? I want to be like them in the adult play world. I just want to say, "Hi, do you want to hang out?" And then have fun.

I also would like to become aware of the times when I set the stage for the falseness in other people to act out. At times I can be a good listener, which sometimes just means that I am a good audience for someone else to parade their ego back and forth across the stage. I add to the insanity of it all by clapping and cheering and throwing bouquets of carnations at their ego's feet, saying, "Oh, you are so successful... Oh, I'm so impressed... Oh, I want to be your friend so I can stand in your spotlight..."

Hmmmm... I feel like someone just showed me the trick behind a grand illusion. I feel like I've been scammed, the fakeness of it all has been revealed and the trick that en-tertained me for so long has lost its appeal. Maybe that's why I enjoy playing with my pets so much, no introductions necessary, playfulness without ego.

Make your ego porous.
Will is of little importance, complaining is nothing, fame is nothing.
Openness, patience, receptivity, solitude is everything.
RAINER MARIA RILKE

I INTEND TO BE AWARE OF THE EGO.

I accept that humanity is plagued by the voice of judgment... *I relinquish* fears of needing to be anything but just plain old perfect me... *I dream of* being Aware... *With peace and love I intend to* see the times when people want to be respected... *I am grateful* to know that we seek from the outside what we are missing on the inside, *I am.*

In a disordered mind, as in a disordered body, soundness of health is impossible.
CICERO

*R*EFLECTIONS ON A PRESCRIPTION FOR HEALTH... Years ago we started searching for treasures around the yard of our nearly 100-year-old home using a metal detector. By the end of the afternoon we had a collection of old medicinal bottles, scraps of metal, and a yard that looked like someone had set off a bunch of landmines. Once again I feel like someone who has discovered a treasure, an Uncle John's Cure-All-That-Ails-You Ointment. But this remedy doesn't come in a bottle.

The aches and pains that have plagued my body for so long have been falling away. No more backaches, no more sore feet, no more pain in my neck, no more grinding of teeth at night, no more tossing and turning trying to find a comfortable position to sleep. So what has been my treasured cure all? Presence. Awareness. Peace. The tension that used to cause me pain was just a physical reflection of my fearful thoughts and emotions. Fear is just a lie. Love is the Truth. Our body is like a lie detector. We respond to lies with stress. Our body sweats, our heart rate increases, our muscles become tense, our blood pressure increases. See the symptoms, look for the lies, relinquish the lies, relinquish the fears... and instead participate in making the choice to Live Beautifully, keep returning to Peace, Love and Acceptance. Choose to live every moment of your life with Truth.

This above all:
to thine own self be true.
WILLIAM SHAKESPEARE

I INTEND TO BE A REFLECTION OF LOVE.

I accept that my physical aches and pains are an indication that I am putting faith in lower realm thoughts... *I relinquish* beliefs in thoughts that result in doubt, worry, unworthiness, and anger... *I dream of* living with Truth... *With peace and love I intend to* be aware that my efforts of aligning my beliefs with Love will result in the Joy of living in a body that is true... *I am grateful* for growing Awareness, *I am.*

If we could give every individual
the right amount of nourishment and exercise,
not too little and not too much,
we would have found the safest way to health.
HIPPOCRATES

EFLECTIONS ON "GIVE US THIS DAY"... As I sat at the table on my porch this morning to a plate of two fried eggs, two pieces of buttered toast, and a glass of orange juice, I was humbled to tears. Before me was a precious gift, a bountiful allotment of nourishment for my body. As I bowed my head in gratitude my tears and emotions flowed not just for my gratitude, but for my humility. How many times in my life had I shoved food into my mouth mindlessly? Not so much as stopping to sit while I took nourishment?

I no longer wish to mindlessly consume. I wish to eat with Gratitude, with Intention. I wish to honor our Earth and eat frugally. I never wish to throw away another scrap of food.

I've missed the boat for so long. No more. I will eat with Love.

The unthankful heart discovers no mercies;
but the thankful heart will find,
in every hour,
some heavenly blessings.
HENRY WARD BEECHER

I INTEND TO BE HUMBLE.

I accept that I have consumed mindlessly... *I relinquish* eating that which harms me and our world... *I dream of* having just the right amount of ideal nourishment for all of us... *With peace and love I intend to* eat food that was grown and transported in a manner that is respectful of our Earthly Mother... *I am grateful* to nourish myself and my family with Love, Honor and Respect, *I am.*

This curious world we inhabit is more wonderful than convenient;
more beautiful than it is useful;
it is more to be admired and enjoyed than used.
HENRY DAVID THOREAU

*R*EFLECTIONS ON THE HEALTH OF OUR WORLD… I stand in awe at the splendid beauty of Nature. Whether I gaze at the intricate beauty of a delicate flower, stand before a majestic oak, or walk along the ocean as the waves crash against the sandy shore, I tremble with awe knowing that I am a part of this magnificent Creation.

I yearn to remain mindful of my Oneness with this beautiful Creation. May I walk gently within this place that we call home. May my presence on this planet add to its splendor and beauty.

I believe that all will be well. There is an Awakening amongst humanity that is stirring our souls to love and care for ourselves, our home, our planet.

I will remain attentive to the possibilities to make the choice to Live Beautifully. I will listen and I will respond.

There is not one blade of grass,
there is no color in this world
that is not intended to make us rejoice.
JOHN CALVIN

I INTEND TO LOVE AND RESPECT CREATION.

I accept that our false sense of separation enables us to treat ourselves and our Earthly Mother poorly… *I relinquish* beliefs in thoughts of separation… *I dream of* humanity being aware of the Oneness of All… *With peace and love I intend to* create only Beauty… *I am grateful* to be a part of this magnificent Creation, *I am.*

Some people grumble that roses have thorns;
I am grateful that thorns have roses.
ALPHONSE KARR

EFLECTIONS ON BEING PRUNED FOR GROWTH... I've gone through a remarkable growth spurt in the past week. Last week I was Chicken Little and this week I feel like Foghorn Leghorn. Last week I was shaking in my boots. Nix that, Chicken Little didn't wear boots. Try again. Last week my feathers were all ruffled over our families' finances. Everywhere I turned there were headlines of doom and gloom. The whole world was going broke. I was frantic. I ran around yelling, "The sky is falling!"

Well, it's a week later and as I sit on my porch and write this, the sun still rises in all its glory. And thankfully I have lost my Chicken Little mentality. So what happened? Reality really hasn't changed too much in a week's time. But my thinking has changed. I accepted that this is the reality of today. And I accepted that it would likely be the reality for some time to come. I could get caught up in feeling like a victim of all the things that I perceived to be 'bad' or I can accept the reality of the day and get on with it. I choose the later.

I choose today to do my work well. I choose to prepare the meals for my family with love and attention to their nutritional needs. I choose to tend to my garden. I choose to gaze at this glorious sunrise. I choose to let the rays of the sun envelop me. I choose to express gratitude for all that is. We are being pruned right now. Cut back. It hurts. I feel bare and exposed. Instead of developing new growth, I feel like it's time for developing a stronger root system. We can each choose to whither and slowly die back or we can choose to refocus our efforts on becoming stronger and healthier than ever before. I choose to focus on inner growth. I will send my roots deep and strong. This growth won't be perceptible in the near future, but in the long run I will grow tall and beautiful.

Better to be pruned to grow than cut up to burn.
JOHN TRAPP

I INTEND TO ACCEPT BEING PRUNED FOR GROWTH.

I accept this pruning... *I relinquish* judging our circumstances... *I dream of* expanding my rootedness... *With peace and love I intend to* send my roots deep into our Mother Earth... *I am grateful* to be aware of my Oneness with Creation, *I am.*

There is no instinct like that of the heart.
LORD BYRON

*R*EFLECTIONS ON TREASURE HUNTING... Today my husband, daughter and I went on a treasure hunt. It took place at our county's fairgrounds at the summer flea market. We set off on our journey unsure of what precious treasures would be found.

We brought home a truckload of everything from an old wool rug for the laundry room, to an old scooter for who knows what, to a crystal light fixture and a vanity to add both bling-bling and function to our daughter's bedroom.

But the biggest treasure of all was a lesson learned. The lady that sold us the vanity told us a story. Earlier this week there was a youth group gathering at her church. The kids wrapped each other in toilet paper mummy style and then had a race across the lawn. This year the kids brought plastic wrap along to get their counselors in on the fun. As they wrapped a counselor his wife stood by observing. She got an uneasy gut-level feeling that this was not good. But the kids were acting with such good intentions that she was reluctant to rain on everyone's picnic, so she held her tongue.

Her husband set off on the race with a spring in his step, but soon lost his footing and began to fall forward. Being bound tightly by the plastic wrap, he had no way of breaking his fall.

He was flown flight for life to a hospital and remains in a coma. He has since developed pneumonia. The family has no health insurance.

The treasure I came home with was the lesson learned... to always trust my gut and to live with Truth by acting on those Instinctual impulses. Our gut feelings provide us with a warning system that has intelligence beyond our mental capacities. We would all be wise to honor it.

Trust instinct to the end, even though you can give no reason.
RALPH WALDO EMERSON

I INTEND TO HONOR MY INSTINCTS.

I accept that I have intelligence beyond my mental capacities... *I relinquish* false beliefs that I need to think everything through... *I dream of* having the wisdom to listen to my Instincts... *With peace and love I intend to* honor my Inner Voice... *I am grateful* to be aware of my Inner Compass, *I am.*

Virtue lies in our power,
and similarly so does vice;
because where it is in our power to act,
it is also in our power not to act...
ARISTOTLE

*R*EFLECTIONS ON LETTING OLD WOUNDS HEAL... Did you ever bite the inside of your cheek and end up with a canker sore? And then were you able to avoid it with your teeth and tongue and allow it to heal or did you unconsciously find yourself biting it and irritating it over and over again only to perpetuate the old sore? Much like dogs who are forced to wear lamp shades on their heads to keep them from obsessively licking their wounds, so too should we humans find ways to stop irritating our own old wounds.

So it goes with me. Old patterns of fearful thinking flare up over and over again. One would think that the logical thing to do would be to recognize the fearful thinking, see it for the useless destructiveness that it is, choose to not listen to it and let the old wounds heal. But the fearful thoughts return to my mind over and over again and without even realizing it I can have picked the sore wide open once again.

As my consciousness grows, so will my capacity to be aware of the reemergence of a fearful thought pattern. I will see them once again and choose to let them pass on by. Thoughts of fear or thoughts of Love? I choose Love.

Sow a thought, and you reap an act;
Sow an act, and you reap a habit;
Sow a habit, and you reap a character;
Sow a character, and you reap a destiny.
SAMUEL SMILES

I INTEND TO BE AWARE OF FEARFUL THOUGHT PATTERNS.

I accept that my faith in habitual negative thought patterns have prevented me from healing... *I relinquish* believing the negative thought patterns... *I dream of* Healing... *With peace and love I intend to* nurture myself to restored health by imagining that I am wearing a lampshade on my head... *I am grateful* to be aware of the effects of shame, doubt, insecurity, unworthiness and anger, *I am.*

I'm late! I'm late!
For a very important date!
No time to say hello, goodbye!
I'm late, I'm late, I'm late!
CHARLES LUTWIDGE DODGSON

*R*EFLECTIONS ON GETTING THERE... Do you remember that crazy rabbit in *Alice in Wonderland* who was obsessed with time? He lived in a frenzy of getting here and there on time. He never seemed to relax in the moment. He never seemed to just Be.

I see myself in that rabbit and in seeing it in another it seems insane. Why spend your life getting there when you are already here? Just Be. I want to enjoy the peace that comes from being where I am. I want to enjoy the peace that comes from accepting life exactly as it is.

I'm not really late,
and I don't really have a date.
I'm a fraud!
CHARLES LUTWIDGE DODGSON

I INTEND TO LIVE PEACEFULLY.

I accept this moment... *I relinquish* fears of needing to get to a better place... *I dream of* knowing that every moment is perfect for the evolution of my soul... *With peace and love I intend to* be observant when I become restless and agitated... *I am grateful* for Life, I am.

We do not suffer by accident.
JANE AUSTEN

REFLECTIONS ON FIXING THE LEAK... When I live with Love, Compassion and Peace, a positive flow of beautiful energy seems to course through my body. I feel energized, yet calm.

At times when I am judgmental, hurt or angry, my energy seems to drain. All that nonsense fearful thinking is like a slow steady leak that when left unchecked is like an all-out draining.

So many of us are fatigued. It is like an unseen plague. There is an anxiety amongst us. An anxiety that we can't seem to fix or get away from. Aches, pains, and fatigue are the physical symptoms of our fearful thoughts and emotions.

In every moment I have the opportunity to experience fear or Love; the suffering from the illusion of separation or the Joy of Union. I wish to see the fearful thoughts for the ugliness that they are. I wish to keep choosing Love over and over again. When I experience Love, I am filled. When I experience fearful thoughts and emotions, I am drained.

I want to listen to my body. Its pain is a message I wish to head. I intend to relinquish the fears. I intend for healing of my mind. I intend to return to Peace and Love.

Love is a choice you make from moment to moment.
BARBARA DE ANGELIS

I INTEND TO BE ENERGIZED BY LOVE.

I accept the messages conveyed to me physically... *I relinquish* beliefs in thoughts of separation... *I dream of* the healing of my mind... *With peace and love I intend to* give up striving out of fear... *I am grateful* to be humble, *I am.*

The destroyer of weeds, thistles, and thorns is a benefactor
whether he soweth grain or not.
ROBERT G. INGERSOLL

REFLECTIONS ON REVEALING THE TREASURES WITHIN... I have spent many hours on my hands and knees pulling garlic mustard from our land. It is a nasty invasive plant that comes up ridiculously early in the spring and shades out hopes of anything else having a chance to grow. I've been weeding with a vengeance dreaming of the day when I would get it under control and then begin the process of going to the garden center and bringing home more desirable plants for my garden.

But now that I have significantly reduced the garlic mustard, what is actually happening is plants and seeds that have remained dormant in the soil for so many years are suddenly experiencing the conditions that they need to grow. There are so many beautiful plants popping up all over the place. It's hard to believe that they were able to remain viable for so long within the soil. This land has been teeming with potential for life that was just waiting for the right circumstances for growth.

I see a parallel in myself. In the relinquishing of my fears (nasty weeds), the creative me can grow. Fears have shaded out my potential for growth. By weeding out the fears, the Light gets through to fertile ground and beautiful growth occurs.

We are not separate from Nature. I see myself reflected in my natural surroundings. Just as the land around me has potential for beautiful creation within its soils, so do I have potential for beautiful creation within myself. All we need are the right conditions. So do the work of pulling and casting off your weeds, shed your fears, the false beliefs that create darkness. Return to Love and experience the growth that comes from living in the Light.

However many years she lived, Mary always felt that 'she should never forget
that first morning when her garden began to grow.'
FRANCES HODGSON BURNETT

I INTEND TO RELEASE ALL THAT BLOCKS MY POTENTIAL FOR LIFE.

I accept that we all have 'weeds'... *I relinquish* fears of needing to be perfect... *I dream of* being aware of fearful beliefs and of doing the work of 'weeding my garden'... *With peace and love I intend to* tend to my inner garden so that I might bloom to my full potential... *I am grateful* to be growing in the Light, *I am.*

*R*EFLECTIONS ON EXCESSIVENESS… Excessive eating results in excessive body mass, which leads to excessive exercise, excessive funds needed to pay for excessive food, excessive forests needed to be cut down for excessive plantings…

I wish to eat simply. I wish to minimize eating food that has required excessive processing, excessive packaging, excessive transportation and excessive cost. I wish to live gently.

I'm finding a new mindset. I will see my excessiveness as an illness of my mind, and thus an illness in my body. I wish to eat simply with respect. I will be kind to myself and thus to our world.

I INTEND TO LIVE SIMPLY.

I accept the effects on my body and on my family's bodies that have resulted from excessive calorie consumption and a lack of good nutrition… *I relinquish* judgment of myself and all others for the error in our ways… *I dream of* my family living with health and vitality… *With peace and love I intend to* honor our bodies by committing myself to making the necessary adjustments in our life to make shopping, cooking and eating a top priority… *I am grateful* to do what is necessary to create a strong foundation for myself and my family, *I am.*

*R*EFLECTIONS ON PREPARATIONS FOR SLUMBER... Our sleep is an important part of our being that we shouldn't overlook. It can be restful and rejuvenating or not. To enjoy a restful night of slumber, let us prepare both ourselves and our bed chambers.

Our evenings are our preparation for slumber. It begins with the meals that we prepare, our reverence for the food that we partake in, the people and the atmosphere that we nourish ourselves with. We need proper illumination; turn off the TV and light the candles.

Our sleep is blissful when we settle our minds before going to sleep. Become joyful, peaceful, quiet, and serene. Build a fire in the fireplace. Read an uplifting book. Play a game. Watch the sunset. Go for a walk. Tend to our homes and our loved ones. Admire the beauty of Nature. Gaze at the moon. Gaze at the stars. Listen to the wind as it rustles the leaves. Prepare our bedroom chambers. Pull back the covers. Dim the lights. Settle into our nests.

True silence is the rest of the mind,
and is to the spirit
what sleep is to the body,
nourishment and refreshment.
WILLIAM PENN

I INTEND TO HONOR MY NEED FOR RESTORATION.

I accept that my body needs to rest and rejuvenate... *I relinquish* fears that manifest as nasty nightmares and discomfort... *I dream of* honoring the need for restoration... *I dream of* having a peaceful mind... *I dream of* having a well-feathered nest... *With peace and love I intend to* nurture myself... *I am grateful* to peacefully slumber, *I am.*

... the love, respect and confidence of my children
was the sweetest reward I could receive for my efforts
to be the woman I would have them copy.
LOUISA MAY ALCOTT

*R*EFLECTIONS ON THE PIED PIPERS... Calling all moms and dads! Calling all aunties and uncles! Calling all grandmas and grandpas! We have a job to do. All hands on deck. Love your children purely. Love their sweet little souls so that they will come to know who they truly are. Focus your love not on their accomplishments, but on their Being. Teach them to quiet their restless minds and experience Joy. Teach them to immerse themselves in the splendid beauty of a sunset, the joy of observing the adventures of the bugs in the backyard or a tiny shoot as it emerges from the earth. Expose them to the joys of Living Beautifully.

How do we teach these things? We teach best by living with Truth. Don't just find a peaceful moment for yourself in your morning meditation, live your entire life in that peaceful moment. If you aren't Living Beautifully every moment of your day, make the choice to find another way. Provide for your family: food, clothing, shelter, education and last, but certainly not least, a life Lived Beautifully.

To Live Beautifully is to live connected to All. To Live Beautifully is to live with Love, Peace, and Joy. To Live Beautifully is to find Acceptance of all that is. Let's walk together, you and me and all our kids. We will be The Pied Pipers who are leading a band of children to a new way of life.

Tell me and I forget,
teach me and I may remember,
involve me and I learn.
BENJAMIN FRANKLIN

I INTEND TO TAKE OTHERS BY THE HAND.

I accept my role as a pied piper... *I relinquish* fears of having enough... *I dream of* a flow of resources that will support joyful expressions of Love... *With peace and love I intend to* show children the joys of choosing to Live Beautifully... *I am grateful* for the blessing of taking others by the hand, *I am.*

*R*EFLECTIONS ON ACCEPTANCE... My lessons of acceptance have increased in magnitude. Finding acceptance in your mother having cancer or your father suffering from a multitude of debilitating health issues seems unnatural. It seems like failure to approach these circumstances with acceptance.

What I've come to realize is that when we cease to be accepting we cut off the Flow. Grace ceases to come through us. And instead the output is a series of negative reactions.

On the contrary, if we are able to be Accepting of what is, the positive flow of Grace seems to flow through us. Thus acceptance doesn't mean that we cease to be active. Acceptance creates the opportunity for Peace and Love to flow in any given moment. That seems like a much better state of being than the option of being paralyzed with fear, like a wide-eyed deer frozen by its focus on the approaching headlights.

A day of worry
is more exhausting than a week of work.
JOHN LUBBOCK

I INTEND TO BE ACCEPTING OF LIFE.

I accept life as it currently is... *I relinquish* fears of this moment being wrong... *I dream of* creating a life of Beauty and Joy... *With peace and love I intend to* relax... *I am grateful* for the affects of Grace, *I am.*

REFLECTIONS ON HOME MAINTENANCE... Get out your tools, friends; we've got work to do! Today we're going to start a home maintenance project. We'll need leak detectors, caulk guns and a good supply of silicone caulk that is guaranteed to create a pressure-tight seal. We will be searching for leaks in our structure and upon finding any we will be caulking up the cracks to prevent any future leakage. Energy is a precious commodity; we need to keep our structures well maintained! The structure I speak of isn't the house that you dwell in, but the body that your soul resides in.

We need to detect leakages. So how do we detect the leakages? Pay attention to whether your reaction to certain circumstances or people in your life leave you feeling drained, depleted and zapped. Some leakages are obvious and others are more subtle. I ask for you to calibrate your leak detectors and to take notice of even the subtlest changes.

Begin by paying attention. Take note of your energy levels. What precedes high energy levels? What precedes low energy levels? What fuels your engine and what chokes it?

The doctor of the future will be oneself.
ALBERT SCHWEITZER

I INTEND TO LIVE WITH AWARENESS OF MY ENERGY.

I accept my physical state... *I relinquish* fears of being affected by what surrounds me... *I dream of* being aware of situations that trigger lower realm responses... *With peace and love I intend to* be aware of whether I am in the lower realm or the Upper Realm... *I am grateful* for awareness of energies, *I am.*

*R*EFLECTIONS ON GRATITUDE... When I feel a little gratitude, I get a little Joy. When I express gratitude abundantly, I get abundant Joy. The two are linked perfectly together. I yearn to open my eyes and my heart to all that I have to be grateful for. I yearn to express gratitude in my journaling, in the stillness of my heart, and to shout it from the rooftops.

The expression of gratitude is like a cleansing. Negative feelings get washed away. My body becomes radiant. With practice gratitude seems to flow effortlessly. I imagine the practice of reflecting on gratitude to the opening of a valve of an old pump. With each feeling of gratitude the valve opens a little more. Feelings of lack turn off the valve.

We all have access to a well of Life that is bursting to flow forth. We are the pump. We must prime the pump so the blessings can flow. Prime the pump with thoughts of gratitude. Each time that we express gratitude we in essence pump the handle. Keep pumping, before long we will have a sparkling fresh flow of Grace. Thoughts of lack and thoughts of deprivation shut down the pump. Rust and muck then clog our lives. Let's choose to be an outlet for Abundance. Be an outlet for the Flow. Let it come through us. The world yearns to be Joyfully Abundant.

All that we are is the result of what we have thought:
all that we are is founded on our thoughts and formed of our thoughts.
If a man speaks or acts with an evil thought, pain pursues him,
as the wheel of the wagon follows the hoof of the ox that draws it.
All that we are is the result of what we have thought:
all that we are is founded on our thoughts and formed of our thoughts.
If a man speaks or acts with a pure thought,
happiness pursues him like his own shadow that never leaves him.
THE DHAMMAPADA

I INTEND TO OPEN MY HEART TO THE FLOW OF GRACE.

I accept the times when the false beliefs of separation perpetuate negativity and lack... *I relinquish* judging Life... *I dream of* Gratitude... *With peace and love I intend to* use acorns as a reminder to be grateful for the potential in my Life... *I am grateful* to be an opening for Grace, *I am.*

Cultivate the habit of being grateful for every good thing that comes to you,
and to give thanks continuously. And because all things have contributed
to your advancement, you should include all things in your gratitude.
RALPH WALDO EMERSON

REFLECTIONS ON MY CHOICE... Our economic reality is different that it was a few short years ago. I want to embrace the change. I refuse to spend my days 'woe is me-ing.' I plan to adapt and move forward. The blessings will be my focus, not my perception of the lack of what once was. My choices will determine whether my life will be one of despair or one of Acceptance and Abundance. Things will be different. But it won't be worse.

Instead of going out for dinner with my husband, we may take a walk and watch a glorious sunset. Instead of shopping for a new toy for our kids, we may dust off the croquet set and head outside for a match. Instead of going to a movie, we may snuggle up next to a fire and read a great book or play a game. I refuse to be poor in spirit. I will keep making the choice to Live Beautifully.

This isn't just a financial matter. It is part of my spiritual practice. The lower realm beliefs of not having enough seek to stay alive and well by identifying with the material things and with wanting and getting. Over and over again I will face the choice of wanting to have or yearning to Be. I will choose to Live Beautifully. I will choose to Be... to be Grateful... to be Joyful... to be Connected. It is sometimes easy to deny the existence of a false belief when it is getting satisfied, but like an unruly toddler it makes itself known when you deny its desires.

Happy is the man who has broken the chains which hurt the mind,
and has given up worrying once and for all.
OVID

I INTEND TO CHOOSE A JOYFUL BEAUTIFUL LIFE.

I accept that wanting creates suffering... *I relinquish* wanting things for the sake of doubt that there will be enough for tomorrow... *I relinquish* wanting things for the sake of feeling worthy of respect and admiration... *I dream of* trusting Life... *With peace and love I intend to* pay attention to my feelings, to my awareness of the emotions that are an indication of whether I suffer from the illusion of separation or am experiencing the joy of Union... *I am grateful* for the joy of creating a beautiful world with Love, *I am.*

Life is a series of natural and spontaneous changes.
Don't resist them; that only creates sorrow.
Let reality be reality.
Let things flow naturally forward in whatever way they like.
LAOZI

ℛEFLECTIONS ON GETTING WHAT YOU ASK FOR... I remember once writing that I wanted to be like a babbling brook. I wanted to be a reflection of Light. Ask and so ye shall receive. I feel like my life lately has been a series of lessons on going with the Flow. I'm learning to not resist what is. I'm learning not to judge situations or people as good or bad, right or wrong. They just are. I'm learning to let go of the outcome and just Be. It is the only choice that ultimately results in Peace.

When I am all by myself surrounded by Nature, it is easy to be in the Flow. Sometimes I struggle in choosing a peaceful loving presence when I am around people. I find myself sucked into a swirl of judgmental thoughts and the resulting emotions and physical tension.

I imagine certain people to be a rock in the middle of the creek bed. I am the babbling brook. I say to myself when I encounter one of these rocks, "Doris, just go with the Flow. Flow right around them. Do not resist their presence. Do not pause to consider thoughts of judgment. Just keep flowing. Just keep being that reflection of Light."

In order for the light to shine so brightly,
the darkness must be present.
FRANCIS BACON

I INTEND TO FLOW WITH ACCEPTANCE OF WHAT IS.

I accept the suffering I experience when I put faith in thoughts of judgment... *I relinquish* believing in the lower realm thinking that plagues my mind... *I dream of* having Awareness when this thought pattern reemerges... *With peace and love I intend to* accept myself and all others exactly as we are in this moment... *I am grateful* to be aware of the falseness of judging, *I am.*

The trip doesn't exist that can set you beyond the reach of cravings,
fits of temper, or fears...
so long as you carry the sources of your troubles about with you,
those troubles will continue to harass and plague you
wherever you wander on land or sea.
LUCIUS ANNAEUS SENECA

REFLECTIONS ON RETOOLING OUR MEDICINE BAGS... My learning to live connected to our Source is a gradual transition. I realize that the striving to get somewhere, the fears, the need for excitement were all just an illness of my mind. As the illness slowly subsides, I have moments where I am able to be in a blissful state of Love and Joy. As the veil slowly dissipates, my vision becomes clearer and the reality I see is beautiful.

We have been sick for so long, that we didn't even know that we were sick. For so long we have lived disconnected from our Source as a result of putting faith in false beliefs.

We need to retool our medicine bags. Awareness of our thinking and connection to our Source are what we need to regain our health.

Ongoing stress creates an energetic environment,
affecting town and country, spreading from nation to nation,
causing disharmony, disease, storms and wars.
The heart's intelligence can help to dissipate these negative energies,
giving people a fresh start in learning how to get along.
As enough people learn about emotional fitness,
it will cause a global shift into new consciousness
that many are talking about,
and then quality of life has a chance of becoming better for the whole.
DOC CHILDRE, AUTHOR OF THE HEARTMATH SOLUTION

I INTEND TO PURSUE WELL BEING.

I accept our illness... *I relinquish* false perceptions of limits to healing... *I dream of* the healing of our minds... *I dream of* the healing of our bodies... *I dream of* the healing of our spirits... *With peace and love I intend to* live with Compassion for myself and for all... *I am grateful* for the gradual lifting of the veil of illusion, *I am.*

An angel can illuminate the thought and mind of man
by strengthening the power of vision.
St. Thomas Aquinas

REFLECTIONS ON ALL THAT SPARKLES CERTAINLY IS GOLD... Did you ever experience a moment that seemed to shine? Did you ever have an idea that seemed to have a special kind of glimmer to it? Did you ever hear another person speak and somehow certain words seemed to have a special message meant just for you?

I think Life sends us Inspirations, little pointers for which way to go. I want to learn to recognize and follow these pointers. I want to honor the Inspirations by acting on them.

The more I follow these Divine Inspirations the more I seem to step into the Flow. When I'm in the Flow, life unfolds swiftly and beautifully. Life is pure sweet joy. There are no struggles.

Plants and animals seem to live in this Flow. Humanity on the other hand seems to have forgotten our union with this Flow somewhere along the way. We can live with Awareness of the Flow or we can live with the illusion of feeling separate and isolated. We can deny that we are a part of this great Whole. That sense of separateness is pure hell. It is the insanity of humanity.

Join with me as I journey towards the Flow. Life will send you signs along the way directing you on your path. Recognize the Sparkles. Follow them. Turn off that brain that wants to overanalyze each decision and just go with it. Follow the Inspirations. Trust your Instincts. Become aware of your Yearnings. Honoring them will lead us to a life of Joy.

A man who works with his hands is a labourer.
A man who works with his hands and his head is a craftsman.
A man who works with his hands,
his head, and his heart is an artist.
St. Francis of Assisi

I INTEND TO RECOGNIZE AND HONOR THE SPARKLES.

I accept that I have unsuccessfully tried to control situations... *I relinquish* beliefs in separation... *I dream of* being aware of the glimmers of Light and of Clarity, the Sparkles... *With peace and love I intend to* honor Guidance... *I am grateful* to be an artist, *I am.*

*R*EFLECTIONS ON TAKING OTHERS BY THE HAND… Before we can begin the work of spiritual growth, our earthly growth must be tended to. Tending to our physical selves with food, clothing and shelter is a necessity. If we desire a peaceful loving world, we must raise our children to be sufficient at caring for themselves and their future families. This will lay the ground work for supporting their spiritual growth.

What makes one person thrive in life and another person struggle to keep a roof over their head? Instability causes fear, doubt and indecision in the child. Faith in these thoughts will not lead the child down the path of success, but one doomed with struggle. When we have thoughts of fear, doubt and indecision, we become people who live lives that are a reflection of that thought. We live lives of failure, poverty and dependence on others.

As families, communities and educators, we need to fill our children's heads with thoughts of safety, security, strength and Love if they are going to live physically healthy lives and thus be in the position to pursue a life of spiritual beauty. Please help to lay this groundwork in your community so that we can live in a little piece of Heaven on Earth.

Let us all search for opportunities to act with strength and confidence
and instill these traits in others.
That which we are, we shall teach, not voluntarily, but involuntarily.
Thoughts come into our minds by avenues which we never left open,
and thoughts go out of our minds through avenues
which we never voluntarily opened.
RALPH WALDO EMERSON

I INTEND TO CREATE A STRONG FOUNDATION FOR MYSELF & MY FAMILY.

I accept that we have strayed from our earthly connection… *I relinquish* fears of sharing from false beliefs of scarcity… *I dream* of being grateful for our Earthly Mother's abundance… *With peace and love I intend to* have a generous spirit… *I am grateful* for the awareness that I am supported in creating the most beautiful life I can possibly imagine, *I am.*

We become
that which we love.
SAINT BRIDGET

*R*EFLECTIONS ON A FLOW... What does it mean to say that one person is more soulful than another? Do some people have more soul than others? Of course not. I think it just means that we can sense their Authenticity more easily. They do not have the blockages that prevent us from experiencing who they truly are. There is a Flow of Loving Energy that ceaselessly comes through them. That is why we flock to these people. We are drawn to the Flow of Energy.

They are like bubbling springs pouring forth an endless supply of Love. Have you ever been walking along in the forest and come upon a spring? It's like there is an opening in the earth from which there is a flow of pure, cold spring water. This is the stuff that beer commercials refer to as 'God's country;' a place where Mother Earth just opens up and flows with pureness.

We too can be springs in God's country. Open your hearts, open your eyes, open your arms and let the Flow of Love come through you. Be a font for all you meet. Nourish each other with the energies you bring forth into this world. Imagine a flow that connects and nourishes us all.

I slept and I dreamed that life is all joy.
I woke and I saw that life is all service.
I served and I saw that service is joy.
KAHLIL GIBRAN

I INTEND TO BE A FLOW OF BEAUTY AND LOVE.

I accept whom I am drawn to... *I relinquish* all that blocks others from experiencing the Authentic me... *I dream of* being an outlet for Love to come into this world... *With peace and love I intend to* honor Heaven by expressing Love on Earth... *I am grateful* for the people in my life that flow with Beauty and Love, *I am.*

In our lives, change is unavoidable, loss is unavoidable.
In the adaptability and ease with which we experience change
lie our happiness and freedom.
BUDDHA

REFLECTIONS ON A LIFELINE... Our son left to go back to college last night. Later in the evening as my husband and I settled into bed I was overcome with sobs. There was an outpouring of so much sadness for days that were no longer to be, so much sadness for the absence of his joyful loving soul in our home. My heart was breaking open as I resented what was and instead desired some precious moment in the past or surely some better days in the future.

When I woke in the morning I decided to turn the tables. What could pull me out from the depths of my despair? Gratitude was my lifeline. I lay in bed thinking of all that I was grateful for in regards to my son going off to college. Instead of dwelling on the past or future, I was completely immersed in gratitude for that very moment exactly as it was. Once again my heart was filled with Acceptance.

We only have now. Unless a walk down memory lane brings you Joy, don't set off on the dream journey. Unless dreams of anticipation of tomorrow bring you Joy, don't go there. Joy. It is available to us in every moment. Take it or leave it.

Let's take it! Let's wrap ourselves in it. Let's open up to it so that we can feel an unending stream of Joy flowing into this world!

A wise man is content with his lot,
whatever it may be,
without wishing for what he has not.
LUCIUS ANNAEUS SENECA

I INTEND TO ACCEPT LIFE.

I accept that the universe is unfolding in a perfectly ever-expanding evolution... *I relinquish* judging any moment to be wrong, bad, or inadequate... *I dream of* making gratitude a habit... *With peace and love I intend to* be open to Joy... *I am grateful* for relaxing and accepting Life, *I am.*

I do not care so much what I am to others
as I care what I am to myself.
MICHEL DE MONTAIGNE

𝓡EFLECTIONS ON ME... I want to be me. I want to be the real Doris Wedige all day today. I want to do only the activities that bring Doris Wedige pure joy. I want to eat only Doris Wedige's favorite foods. I want to wear my favorite clothes and my favorite jewelry.

I am so grateful for my life exactly as it is. I don't want to be anyone but me. I don't want to be like anyone but me in any regard. I don't want anyone else's talents, tastes, economic status, or their body. I just want to be me.

I am accepting exactly who I am, how I am, & what I am. I am who I am and I am perfect. I am grateful to be in the skin I'm in!

As soon as you trust yourself,
you will know how to live.
JOHANN WOLFGANG VON GOETHE

I INTEND TO EMBRACE MY TRUE NATURE.

I accept that I have doubted that I was created with perfection... *I relinquish* judging myself to be inadequate... *I dream of* accepting each of us as we are at this moment... *With peace and love I intend to* grow with Compassion... *I am grateful* to be perfectly uniquely authentically me, *I am.*

And what is a man without energy?
Nothing – nothing at all.
MARK TWAIN

*R*EFLECTIONS ON LEAKS IN THE DAM... Imagine yourself to be the Hoover Dam; that great wall of cement that holds a vast amount of energy behind it. Now imagine that cement wall to have leaks. Holes in the cement where the vital energy source spews though. Imagine more and more of these cracks. More and more leakages of water. With each leakage the force behind the wall lessens.

So it is with our own being. The incessant thinking of our brains creates energy leaks. Left unchecked our brains can entertain themselves with a relatively constant flow of energy-draining thought. Useless replays of the past and useless worry over the future create holes that deplete us of vital energy.

Have you ever found yourself worn out from worry of your future or worn out from carrying the burden of your past? Shore up the holes large and small. Be aware of your incessant thinking. Get out those caulk guns and shore up the holes. Awareness is your caulk gun. Awareness is all you need to patch up the holes. Be the keeper of your dam. Observe your thinking, seek awareness of the leaks.

For one who has conquered the mind,
the mind is the best of friends;
but for one who has failed to do so,
the mind will remain the greatest enemy.
THE BHAGAVAD-GITA

I INTEND TO LIVE WITH AWARENESS OF THE MIND.

I accept that the mind is often full of negative thought patterns that give the illusion of separation... *I relinquish* believing the fears, the doubts and the judgments that plague my mind... *I dream of* having awareness of thoughts of regret for the past or frets over the future... *With peace and love I intend to* focus on my breath for a few moments when I am aware of the onset of negative thinking... *I am grateful* for the serenity that comes when I cease to believe every thought that enters my mind, *I am.*

REFLECTIONS ON BEING EXQUISITELY ALIVE... I feel like a flower in the garden; unthinking and yet exquisitely alive and well. Without the aid of a brain for thought, the flowers in my garden grow and blossom. They draw from the earth all that nourishes them and they turn to the light as the sun crosses the sky. They function and live without ever a thought. But they do appear to me to experience different states of being. Flowers in my garden sometimes appear to be affected by too much or too little. Too much rain, not enough rain... Other times the flowers in my garden appear to be downright vibrant and joyful!

Sometimes during meditation I feel like I am a flowering plant in a garden. I experience my body alive and moving. I experience the Source of All without thinking a single thought.

One might think that to turn off our brains we might wither up, but I have found the opposite to be true. Only in the turning off of our brains can we become aware of Life and truly Live Beautifully.

If I ever cross paths with a scare crow declaring, "If I only had a brain," I will be sure to let him know that having a brain isn't all that it's cracked up to be. I will encourage him to reconsider his pursuit of a brain and instead just continue on his journey down the yellow brick road in his joyful scarecrow fashion.

Stop thinking,
and end your problems.
LAOZI

I INTEND TO BE AWARE.

I accept that I have denied much of my potential for growth... *I relinquish* believing that life is a struggle... *I dream of* quieting my restless mind and surrendering to the Flow of Life... *With peace and love I intend to* quiet myself in hopes of sensing that which transforms acorns into oaks... *I am grateful* for the Joy of Life that awaits for my choosing, *I am.*

𝓡EFLECTIONS ON 'MY HAIR IS NOT PURPLE'… One day I was making dinner when I got a phone call. My girlfriend was frantic. Her husband had come home from work and had accused her of all sorts of horrible shortcomings. She was distraught. The person who was suppose to love her unconditionally had revealed that he believed that in some regards she was not worthy of respect. Her heart was broken and she crumbled in a flood of tears and emotions. As we spoke I was furious with her husband. After we hung up I stood there washing the dishes and it occurred to me that all he had said was a lie and that we had believed him.

I called her back and told her that I didn't think that her purple hair was attractive. I told her that it was downright ugly. She was completely bewildered. She confidently responded with "What are you talking about? My hair is NOT purple."

I was silent for a moment and then asked her why she didn't respond to the falseness of her husband's comments in the same way. We talked about how at some level she had to have believed what he had said. When she didn't believe me, it didn't evoke a lower realm response. The lie just simply was recognized as such, and fell flat. There was no flood of fearful thoughts and emotions.

Since then 'My hair is not purple' has become our mantra when her or I are faced with someone judging us and telling us a lie either through their words, their actions or their attitudes. It is a reminder to stay strong in our Truth. It is a reminder to be so strong in our convictions of what is true about ourselves, that other people cannot affect us. 'My hair is not purple' has become our shield that protects us from being injured by the sword of judgment.

What people believe prevails over truth.
SOPHOCLES

I INTEND TO PROTECT MYSELF FROM LIES.

I accept that we are plagued with falseness… *I relinquish* looking to others for validation… *I dream of* responding to lies with an awareness of Truth… *With peace and love I intend to* respond to judgments with "My hair is not purple"… *I am grateful* to take up the shield of Awareness, *I am.*

*R*EFLECTIONS ON BEING CENTERED... What is it that people mean when they say that they feel centered? Or out in left field? Or out of kilter? Or out of sync?

My daughter gave me a Gap t-shirt that says 'centered' on the front. I wear it on days when I'm feeling as though everything is right in the world.

I think being centered means standing right at the hub of the wheel, while a beautiful yin-yang of Heaven and Earth spin on an axis around me. I stand centered in stillness in the midst of so much movement. So much Life.

I like it here on the hub. I need to remember this place, so when I find myself experiencing one of those days where I feel like I'm spinning out of control, like I'm the little white ball that's been thrown onto the spinning roulette wheel, being jarred and thrown this way and that, I just need to jump on the hub... and enter the Stillness in the spinning wheel of Life.

I INTEND TO EXPERIENCE STILLNESS IN THE MIDST OF LIFE.

I accept what is... *I relinquish* judgment of all that I perceive... *I dream of* experiencing the Stillness in the fullness of Life... *With peace and love I intend to* stand on the hub not denying what spins around me, but finding Stillness in the Acceptance and Love of all that is... *I am grateful* for Life, *I am.*

Mostly it is loss which teaches us about the worth of things.
ARTHUR SCHOPENHAUER

ℛEFLECTIONS ON A SHIFT… Something is shifting inside of me. I seem to be doing things from a different place. It's not that what I'm doing has changed, but the power of origin is changing. I seem to be living from a place of Powerful Love, instead of a place of victimization.

I started to be aware of how I see myself as a victim in certain situations. Like the petals of an opening flower the many aspects of my life where I have played the part of the victim are slowly revealing themselves to me. My relationship in my birth family, victim; my relationship with my own family, victim; my relationship with the world as a woman, victim; my relationship with our health care system, victim.

It's a beautiful thing to see yourself for how you are. In the seeing it with eyes that are nonjudgmental, a shift occurs. It's like once you see it without naming it good or bad, right or wrong; there is no going back. The change has begun. Awareness is a Light that heals.

I see myself clearly. I accept myself. Now I will choose over and over to return to my birthplace of Love and Power. I no longer wish to dwell in the hell that I have created that is a place of fear and victimization. And when I do repeat my patterns of being a victim, when I replay the old stories in my head of the times that I believe I have been wronged, I will stop and see with Compassionate eyes. And then, once again, let it fall away.

To be yourself in a world that is constantly trying to make you something else is the greatest accomplishment.
RALPH WALDO EMERSON

I INTEND TO BE AWARE OF THE FALSENESS OF BEING A VICTIM.

I accept that I perpetuate fearful thoughts of being a victim… *I relinquish* unhealthy patterns of thought… *I dream of* Healing… *With peace and love I intend to* live with Strength… *I am grateful* for realizing that there is power in my choice, *I am*… *I am grateful* to be Aware, *I am.*

To poke a wood fire is more solid enjoyment
than almost anything else in the world.
CHARLES DUDLEY WARNER

REFLECTIONS ON DAYS IN THE SUN… At the end of our vacation last summer I vowed I was going to spend as much time as possible camping in the following year. Here I am in the next year and so far I haven't camped a single day. So how do I get that camping-in-the-great-outdoors state of being wherever I am?

Camping is a large dose of nature, water, blue skies, and campfires. Camping is life without 'work.' Of course, there are plenty of things to tend to, but they don't feel like they carry the negative 'work' load.

Simplicity. Limited schedules. Less time running. Limited stuff. Less time spent caring for the stuff. More time spent caring for the soul. Simple, but nourishing food. Dining al fresco. Relaxed time in the company of friends and family.   Coffee clutches on the shore as the sun rises. Gathering for meals. Gathering for sunbathing. Gathering around the campfire.

Camping means activities that are, but would never be called, exercise. Long bike rides to town for ice cream, hikes up cliffs and through the forest, strolls along the shoreline, kayaking across the lake to the island. Activities for the sake of Joy, not for exercise. Living in the great outdoors is a recipe for health, both physical and soulful: nature, simplicity, camaraderie, physical exertion, tending to life.

So why do I live this way for just a short period of time each year? None of it is expensive and limited to the rich. It's because I've chosen to live my life differently.

Now begins a new day. I will choose to create a life of Joy!

If one keeps loving faithfully what is really worth loving,
and does not waste one's love on insignificant and unworthy and meaningless things,
one will get more light by and by and grow stronger.
VINCENT VAN GOGH

I INTEND TO UNPLAN MY LIFE.

I accept that I have complicated my life with activities that bring me down… *I relinquish* fears of change… *I dream of* a life of Joy… *With peace and love I intend to* unplan my life… *I am grateful* to choose wisely, *I am.*

REFLECTIONS ON YEARNING TO BE... I've worked so hard to have so much. But now the having is losing its appeal. It now feels like obligations and stuff that weighs me down and prevents me from living the life I yearn for. I yearn to simply Be. To be Still. To be Peaceful. To be Joyful. To be Open. To be Compassionate.

I'm finding having getting in the way of Being. I have too many obligations. I have too much guilt. I have too much stuff to clean, maintain and pay for.

To create the space to Be, I will respond to choices that support it. I will keep responding to life by choosing the option of Being and choosing to undo obligations that hinder it. I desire to keep making the choice to Live Beautifully. I choose to simply Be.

I INTEND TO BE.

I accept when having serves to temporarily satisfy fearful desires... *I accept* that my spirit thrives on Being... *I relinquish* fears of letting go of things that I once thought had value... *I dream of* having eyes that see when I seek distraction from discomfort through getting more stuff... *With peace and love I intend to* make the choice to Live Beautifully... *I am grateful* to be open to change, *I am.*

I would rather be what God chose to make me
than the most glorious creature that I could think of;
for to have been thought about,
born in God's thought,
and then made by God,
is the dearest, grandest and most precious thing in all thinking.
GEORGE MACDONALD

REFLECTIONS ON BEING FRUITFUL... It has been pure joy to have been born a woman and been given the chance to experience the creation of a life within me. To have birthed a creation is miraculous.

Life in any form grows and unfolds. I feel a connectedness with the plants in my garden. They can grow lush and green, bud, bloom, bear fruit, disperse seed and then slowly recede back to the earth. I feel as though I am a reflection of them and them of me.

My children are growing, they are expanding, growing greener and more lush with every season, but at this time the buds are tight. I look on with joyful anticipation of their flowering. Oh, they are like packages under the Christmas tree, I want to dive in and open them all to reveal their contents, but alas I must be patient and wait for their gentle unfolding. Wait for them to bloom in their own due time and reveal the exquisiteness of their own authentic expressions of creation.

Earth's crammed with heaven...
But only he who sees, takes off his shoes.
ELIZABETH BARRETT BROWNING

I INTEND TO BE AWARE OF MY AUTHENTICITY.

I accept the gifts that have come through me... *I relinquish* expectations of how they will be... *I dream of* having a heart that flows with Love, Compassion and Bounty... *With peace and love I intend to* cherish authenticity... *I am grateful* for the Life that flows through me, *I am.*

The garden is a metaphor for life, and gardening is a symbol of the spiritual path.
LARRY DOSSEY, M.D.

REFLECTIONS ON PLAYING IN THE DIRT... After a long cold winter, spring has arrived in all its splendor. I can at last get outside and "play in the dirt" as my grandma says. In the winter I would spend hours paging through seed catalogs dreaming of the possibilities of what I could grow in my garden. It's really quite amazing, relatively similar little seeds will produce a wide variety of results.

I've been tending a new sort of garden these days; my life. I wish to grow plants that will produce fruits and vegetables for nourishment and plants that will produce flowers for pure Joy. And all important is the space between the plants for cultivating Stillness and for movement of the Breath of Life. So where do we find the seeds for the gardens of our lives? We find them in our imaginations. Our inspired thoughts are the seeds; they are Inspiration for creating beauty in our lives. The Inspirations that we choose to honor with intention are the seeds that we choose to plant in our gardens.

The seed catalog of life has so many possibilities. Open yourself to dream. Honor the Inspirations by intending them to be. Follow through with a spirit of Gratitude, Delight, and Love. These energies are like gentle rainfall on our gardens. Follow up with an abundance of Joy, for Joy is like sunshine. Soon our gardens will be sprouting all that we have planted. Keep tending to your creations with the energy that brings life, Love. Occasionally, dark moments will come with judgments, fears and doubts that will manifest in your garden as nasty weeds. Don't fret, gently pull the weeds and throw them on the compost pile.

My garden is my most beautiful masterpiece.
CLAUDE MONET

I INTEND TO CULTIVATE BEAUTY.

I accept that I receive Inspirations... *I relinquish* the habit of putting faith in the fearful thoughts that inevitably follow the Inspirations... *I dream of* the knowing to settle into my bones that our Earthly Mother delights in bringing forth our Heavenly Father's inspirations... *I dream of* grace and wisdom as I choose to honor the Inspirations... *I am grateful* to be Creative, *I am.*

There has been much tragedy in my life;
at least half of it actually happened.
MARK TWAIN

*R*EFLECTIONS ON CHOOSING HOW TO CULTIVATE... Once we have planted our gardens we must become the watchers. Fears will come. Fears are like weeds in our gardens. We must become astute observers so that we recognize these weeds, thereby stunting their growth before they have the chance to grow and multiply and take over our gardens. Just as a gardener trains herself to recognize the little seedlings that pop up so that she can pull the weeds while they are still small, so too must we train ourselves to recognize our fearful thought patterns and banish them while they are still small.

I dream of the day when we join hands in our garden, when we dance with Joy amidst the dew and the sunshine. Join me here. Join me in our Garden. Our Garden of Eden is here.

The great many gardens of the world,
of literature and poetry,
of painting and music,
of religion and architecture
all make the point as clear as possible:
The soul cannot thrive in the absence of a garden.
THOMAS MORE

I INTEND TO BANISH DOUBT.

I accept that thoughts of anxiety, doubt and judgment inevitably follow thoughts that are Inspired... *I relinquish* believing every thought that occurs on my mind... *I dream of* discerning between the Inspired thoughts of the Upper Realm (Grace/Union) and the fearful thoughts of the lower realm (ego/separation)... *With peace and love I intend to* honor Inspiration with Intention and Faith... *I am grateful* to know that Heaven and Earth rejoice when I choose to cultivate Beauty, *I am.*

Bad habits are like a comfortable bed,
easy to get into,
but hard to get out of.
ENGLISH PROVERB

*R*EFLECTIONS ON TAKING CHARGE... My thoughts have been like Grand Central Station. I'm exhausted from all of the activity. I've decided to employ a conductor. All thoughts must meet strict criteria or they will be met with an out-thrust hand and forced to recede.

I am the conductor. No more rambling on of pointless thoughts. If I choose to think about something, so be it. I will think as necessary, and then turn off the machine.

If willy-nilly thoughts of the past or worries of the future pop up, 'The Conductor' will immediately discharge them from the train before they have a chance to upset the peace and stillness of my first-class high-speed luxurious train car.

I'm in charge now. I've come to know moments of Peacefulness and I wish to live in the Bliss 24-7. The Bliss is a choice I will make by choosing to turn off the mental static and choosing to open my mind to receive Inspiration.

Consciousness creates the body, pure and simple.
Consciousness isn't just in the head.
It is far more vast than your brains and bodies
and exists beyond time and space.
On a practical day-to-day level, however,
our consciousness is the part of us that chooses and directs our thoughts.
Thoughts that are uplifting, nurturing and loving
create healthy biochemistry and healthy cells
while thoughts that are destructive to self and to others do just the opposite.
CHRISTIANE NORTHRUP, M. D.

I INTEND TO HAVE AWARENESS OF DAMAGING THOUGHT.

I accept that much of humanity is plagued with incessant fearful thinking... *I relinquish* worrying... *I dream of* my mind being Healed... *With peace and love I intend to* have a peaceful, joyful presence... *I am grateful* to be aware of my mind, *I am.*

Write the bad things that happen to you in the sand,
but write the good things that happen to you on a piece of marble.
ARABIC PROVERB

REFLECTIONS ON FORGIVENESS... Why do we say "Let it go" when we speak of forgiveness or "Why are you holding on to the past?" It sounds as if we are talking about something physical, not just a thought or memory held in our brains. Are we letting go of a memory? No, we still remember. It's more like when we decide to truly forgive there is a physical letting go that happens along with the emotional letting go.

It's like the cells in our body have a memory all their own. When we forgive the tightness falls away from our bodies. True forgiveness seems to facilitate an opening, a release of the physical baggage we carry in our cells. Forgiveness seems to literally lighten our load.

To be wronged is nothing,
unless you continue to remember it.
CONFUCIUS

I INTEND TO BE FORGIVING.

I accept that people hurt each other... *I accept* that I have been hurt and that I have hurt others... *I relinquish* wishing for things to have been different than how they have been... *I dream of* Love flowing into the places within me where I once held on to pain... *I dream of* Healing for those I have hurt... *With peace and love I intend to* let go of judgment... *I am grateful* to be aware of the cleansing that is available to us, *I am.*

If the sight of the blue skies fills you with joy,
if a blade of grass springing up in the fields has power to move you,
if the simple things of nature have a message that you understand,
rejoice,
for your soul is alive.
ELEANORA DUSE

*R*EFLECTIONS ON PURITY... I hold in my hand, close to my heart, two dying chicks. They have been with us just a few short days, but the beauty of their lives can't be measured by its length.

Sunny hatched on a Thursday evening and was an immediate delight and favorite of the entire family. You couldn't help but smile and feel joyful looking at his sweet little bright eyes against a ball of yellow fluff. Although his legs never allowed him to move about, he lay on his back and welcomed an exchange of Love and Joy from all who came his way.

How is it that I can be crying such tears for a wee little creature that just hatched a few short days ago? Because I have loved him so purely. So many human relationships are plagued with lower realm wants and needs. The love I felt for this chick has been a pure joyful love.

I give thanks for dear sweet Sunny. He has taught me so much. I pray that I can see the same Innocence in my fellow mankind that I so easily saw in Sunny.

When we see men of worth,
we should think of equaling them;
when we see men of a contrary character,
we should turn inward and examine ourselves.
CONFUCIUS

I INTEND TO SEE INNOCENCE.

I accept that I often fail to see Innocence in my fellow man... *I relinquish* the fears and judgments that obscure my seeing our Truth... *I dream of* having Compassionate eyes... *With peace and love I intend to* look within when I judge others harshly... *I am grateful* for flowers, kitty cats and chicks, *I am.*

Hatred does not cease by hatred, but only by love;
this is the eternal rule.
BUDDHA

*R*EFLECTIONS ON RETURNING TO LOVE... Love, forgiveness, acceptance... I've said these words so many times before, but I'm feeling like I'm seeing them anew. I used to save the concept of forgiveness for things I considered big. Situations that I judged to be big misdoings seemed to warrant forgiveness. I'm beginning to see situations not as good or bad but just as the absence or presence of Love. Forgiveness clears up the repetitive unhealthy patterns that have been put into place whenever there has been an act of fear.

I realize how many moments in my life that I've chosen to live without Love. Every moment that we choose to not love entirely, whatever the experience may be, is a moment of darkness instead of Light.

Our minds judge some moments to be bigger than others. But really they're not. Just another moment to Live Beautifully, to be Loving, to be Accepting, to be Joyful or another moment to not. To not, and instead to resist, to be rigid, to judge, to regret (to fall under the illusion of separation).

Often times we believe we are justified in calling ourselves a victim. When in fact we're just holding on to judging a moment when there was an absence of Love... choosing to judge, choosing to remain resentful. Where do we draw the line on what is forgivable? Is it honorable to forgive your neighbor and hate your body? When is anything but Love our choice? Love is Love, fear is fear, hate is hate, judgment is judgment; the energy is the same regardless of what it's directed towards.

I am not afraid of storms,
for I am learning to sail my ship.
LOUISA MAY ALCOTT

I INTEND TO ENJOY THE BLISSFUL FREEDOM OF FORGIVENESS.

I accept the falseness of wanting to hold on to the past... *I relinquish* wishing for anything to have been different than what it has been... *I dream of* Healing... *With peace and love I intend to* let go of regret... *I am grateful* for the flow of Grace that seeps into the places where I once held onto pain, *I am.*

*R*EFLECTIONS ON STICKY TRANSITIONS... When the theme song from our son's junior prom comes on the radio it takes me back to a magical moment of watching him and his classmates in a choreographed dance in the high school gymnasium. Midway through the song there is a shift. The dancers, the audience, we all hear it, feel it; an awkward change in the beat. We all must make a transition.

I love that song. It was so fitting for their prom. To me the song reflected the transition of stepping out of childhood and into early adulthood. The beat in the first half of the song is pleasant as well as the different beat in the second half. It's the transition that feels sticky.

If I had a theme song for this moment in my life, it too would have a shift in the beat. I am experiencing a change. My old ways are out of sync. I'm choosing a new way of Being. A new beat.

My theme song would begin with highs and lows, sorrows and excitements, and then the dancer would be forced to hold her bent leg suspended while the music transitioned to a new steady beat, a song of Exuberance, Peace, Love and Joy.

I INTEND TO EMBRACE CHANGE.

I accept transitions that seem sticky... *I relinquish* fears of changes... *I dream of* Grace as my life unfolds... *With peace and love I intend to* embrace each and every transition... *I am grateful* for the movement in my life, *I am.*

Peace comes from within.
Do not seek it without.
BUDDHA

*R*EFLECTIONS ON MAKING A CHOICE… Our attention to anything adds to it. Our thoughts are energy. So when we think of something we are adding to 'it' whatever that may be. 'Spread the word' strengthens it.

Emotions are like super-charged thoughts. Mega-energy. So if you are emotional, you add to whatever you're thinking about. If you get 'really emotional,' you get really energized over something. Every thing, thought, and emotion are all energy.

So by directing our thoughts and emotions we direct our energy to strengthen what we wish. We have the power to create by choosing our thoughts and emotions. Strengthen the Love in this world with thoughts, emotions and acts of Love. Strengthen the peace in this world with thoughts, emotions and acts of Peace.

See the falseness of the lower realm thoughts that plague our minds. Our belief in them is the source of our lower realm emotions. See how putting faith in those thoughts holds us back from taking the next step on our Live Beautifully Journey. See the thoughts and emotions that create darkness and despair. Our awareness of the lower realm will lead to its demise.

World peace is really very simple—each of us choosing Love. If we live with Love, we create Peace. If we continue to entertain thoughts of fear, we experience pain and suffering. If we believe in the fearful thoughts and choose to fight injustice, we choose fear, we choose pain.

Treat people as if they were what they ought to be,
and you'll help them to become what they are capable of becoming.
JOHANN WOLFGANG VON GOETHE

I INTEND TO BE A PROLIFIC CREATOR OF PEACE AND LOVE.

I accept the world as it is at this moment… *I relinquish* judging humanity for our failures… *I dream of* healing for us all… *With peace and love I intend to* create a beautiful life… *I am grateful* to be aware of my power to create Beauty, *I am.*

You are an alchemist; make gold of that.
WILLIAM SHAKESPEARE

*R*EFLECTIONS ON A TRANSFORMATION... For years I was plagued by PMS. Every month I transformed from sweet likeable Doris to a churning ugly monster that neither I nor anyone else liked to be around. As my Awareness grew I began to observe the aches, pains & nasty thoughts and emotions. Month after month I would experience this dark cloud. I decided to just observe it.

Then one fine day my family was gathered together for the holidays making cut-out cookies. As I sat on the kitchen stool, I felt 'it' coming. I quickly excused myself and told my family that I wanted to take a catnap. I crawled into bed and became acutely aware. I could feel a darkness within me. With every bit of attention focused on this energy, I felt its movement within me. I didn't think about it, I just was very aware of it. The more I observed it the denser it became. I stayed with it as it became denser and denser in my abdomen. It was like it got smaller and denser until it imploded. Now I realize that PMS is the onset of a cycle of old energies that come up and seek to be fed the low energies that support their survival. Fortunately, we have the ability to weaken darkness with the Light of Awareness.

If you or someone you love experiences this, begin by observing. Get a calendar, chart your cycle. Record how you feel every day. Number the days beginning with one on the first day of the menstrual cycle. You may begin to see a pattern of when the darkness will descend. Open up those days in your schedule if you can. Allow yourself the rest you need as you physically and emotionally deal with the darkness. Sit in meditation and become aware. When the darkness comes up have a 'stare down' of sorts. Focus every bit of your awareness on it. Your awareness leads to its demise. Month after month weaken it a little more with your awareness.

The strongest principle of growth lies in human choice.
GEORGE ELIOT

I INTEND TO TRANSFORM DARKNESS WITH LIGHT.

I accept femininity and all of the history that comes with it... *I relinquish* fears of the darkness that rears its ugliness premenstrually... *I dream of* transforming this darkness into Light... *With peace and love I intend to* accept life exactly as it is... *I am grateful* to be free of blockages, *I am.*

*R*EFLECTIONS ON OUR MATERNAL INSTINCT... As women we often are fine tuned to our loved one's health. We know that too much of this will upset Johnnie's stomach, we know when Susie is starting to feel a little run down from a cold that's coming on. We detect the slightest disturbances in our family's physical health and make adjustments along the way to ward off an illness.

I sense a new aspect of parenting coming on. I think we will become finely tuned machines in detecting our family's pain bodies. Will we make the same efforts to keep pain bodies at bay as we do to keep colds and the flu at bay?

Will we know what circumstances seem to trigger our loved ones' pain bodies? Will we sense the stirrings early on and warn our child of it? Will "don't fuel your pain body" become as quick to roll off our tongues as "cover your mouth when you sneeze?" Will we say things like "feed a cold, starve a pain body?" Will teachers be trained to recognize and deal appropriately with their students' pain bodies?

I want to become an acute observer of myself and my family. I want to be able to detect the triggers that stir my own pain body as well as those of my family. I want to help them to recognize both mine and their own triggers. It initially might be easier for them to see it in me than in themselves. I want my family to learn to become intensely Present in those moments and thus ward off a full-blown pain body attack.

I wish I could show you,
when you are lonely or in darkness,
the astonishing light of your own Being.
HAFIZ

I INTEND TO BE AWARE OF THE PAIN BODY TRIGGERS.

I accept that we all carry old pain... *I relinquish* fears of suffering from the effects of someone else's pain body... *I dream of* being Aware of pain body triggers... *With peace and love I intend to* be compassionate when a person is overcome by a hungry pain body... *I am grateful* to recognize the pain body and to respond to it with Love, *I am.*

Conviction is worthless
unless it is converted into conduct.
THOMAS CARLYLE

REFLECTIONS ON THE SEEDS TO SOW... Your thoughts are seeds in your garden. Choose to be the maker of your sanctuary, your garden. Choose the seeds and you will ultimately choose the growth, the blossoms. If you find yourself thinking thoughts aligned with fear, worry, doubt, lack, judgment or anger, stop and know that if you continue these thoughts, these 'seeds,' will become the plants that will bloom in your garden. You are the maker of your landscape. Choose your thoughts today and in doing so you sow the seeds for tomorrow. Look around and observe your circumstances and know that it is a result of how you have thought, how you have been. Accept what is, then make the choice to take another step on the Live Beautifully Journey.

You are not a victim of circumstance. You are a creator of circumstance. Choose wisely on behalf of our human family.

Everything is gestation and then bringing forth.
To let each impression and each germ of a feeling
come to completion wholly in itself,
in the dark, in the inexpressible, the unconscious,
beyond the reach of one's own intelligence,
and await with deep humility and patience the birth-hour of a new clarity:
that alone is living the artist's life,
in understanding and in creating.
RAINER MARIA RILKE

I INTEND TO CREATE WITH LOVE.

I accept that we are a reflection of what we have thought... *I relinquish* all thought that makes me feel bad... *I dream of* having Awareness of the energies that are created by my thoughts... *With peace and love I intend to* choose thoughts that create with Love... *I am grateful* for having eyes that see, *I am.*

*R*EFLECTIONS ON A BAD DREAM... I had a nightmare last night. I got into my car and put it in drive to pull away from a curb on the left side of the road. Instead of going forward the car moved backwards. No matter what I did, I moved backwards. In my rearview mirror I could see flashing red lights and emergency vehicles. I came to a stop amongst the vehicles in front of a house. I watched in horror as a man with many wives and children abused himself and the women. He inserted long needles into his leg muscle until it entered the bone. Then he twisted the needles.

I was drawn into the situation to protect the children, to care for the women. We were completely stressed trying to deal with his insanity and keep a somewhat normal life for the children. We were constantly changing to satisfy that monster of a man so that he might not lash out at one of us. We never thought of leaving. I'm not sure why. I think we couldn't abandon each other and there were so many of us and we were so terrorized all the time that we couldn't get our thoughts together for long enough to make a plan.

That horrible man attempted to keep us in that place by creating horror and fear in an effort to control us. By not allowing for us to have a peaceful moment, the necessary first step to realizing anything, he kept us there with him. By creating circumstances that influenced our thoughts and emotions, he attempted to keep us from being free, from being creators of a new and different reality. We must give ourselves and our children the gift of freedom. Freedom from fearful thought. As we free ourselves from the grips of fear, we Live Beautifully.

Concern should drive us into action and not into a depression.
No man is free who cannot control himself.
PYTHAGORAS

I INTEND TO WALK AWAY FROM UNLOVING CIRCUMSTANCES.

I accept that the darkness controls with thoughts of fear... *I relinquish* thoughts that I am unworthy of Love... *I dream of* having the wisdom to walk away from darkness... *With peace and love I intend to* nurture myself to wellness and pray for those who live without Love... *I am grateful* to know that I can pray and get out of the way, *I am.*

REFLECTIONS ON QUIETING THE MONSTER... Quiet that voice in your head, that voice named fear, that evil monster that keeps us frozen and terrorized. The one that controls us by keeping us so focused merely on survival that we don't have time to think of anything else. Quiet it by observing it, by naming it, by identifying it despite the many disguises it wears. Sometimes our loved ones are possessed by this monster. It may try to get to you through them. Look it straight in the face and recognize it. Your on-going awareness of it slowly makes it recede to nothingness.

When you have succeeded in diminishing it, Peace creeps in; a beautiful tranquil Peace that allows for you to have the freedom to choose your own thoughts. Your reality begins with your own thinking and so by clearing the space within your mind that was occupied by the lower realm thinking you then have the capacity to gently choose your thoughts with care.

Think beautifully. Think thoughts of acceptance, love, beauty and grace and you will be Accepting, Loving, Beautiful and Graceful. Your Being, that which you are, creates an attraction. It attracts likeness to you. It attracts like people, like circumstances. Birds of a feather flock together. Do not wish for the life you want. Be as you desire to Be. Ignore that voice in your head, choose your thoughts, and open your mind, your heart and arms to receive the Grace that comes when you make the choice to Live Beautifully.

It will never rain roses:
when we want to have more roses,
we must plant more roses.
GEORGE ELIOT

I INTEND TO THINK AS I DESIRE TO BE.

I accept that sometimes there is a voice in my head... *I relinquish* the habit of believing the negative thoughts... *I dream of* Healing... *With peace and love I intend to* Live Beautifully... *I intend to* think beautiful thoughts... *I intend to* express beautiful emotions... *I am grateful* to release controlling my life out of fear, *I am*... *I am grateful* to create my life with Love, *I am*... *I am grateful* to settle into the flow of Life that turns acorns into oaks, *I am*.

We shall find peace.
We shall hear angels.
We shall see the sky sparkling with diamonds.
ANTON CHEKOV

REFLECTIONS ON TOO MUCH NOISE... Sometimes it's very difficult to get my kids' attention. They can be listening to music, talking on the phone, watching TV and chatting with a dozen people on Facebook *all* at the same time. It's no wonder they don't hear me. It can be very frustrating. I can't help but wonder if it is a healthy way for them to be. Whatever happened to having a conversation with one person at a time or maybe even a solitary moment? Oh, the woes of being a parent in the 21st century!

I wonder if our guardian angels feel the same frustration. Are they trying to get our attention, trying to advise us on the way to go, only to have the messages fall on overly-distracted ears? Is the incessant voice in our heads so persistent that we rarely experience a moment of peacefulness in which we might 'feel' a Nudge or 'see' a Sparkle?

Does the voice in our heads that drones on and on over the dilemma of the day drown out the Inspired thoughts that we really want to hear? Do we honor our intellect more than the Knowings?

With age, wisdom returns, the wisdom to listen, the wisdom to honor Inspiration, the wisdom to intend for Healing.

The closer one approaches to God,
the simpler one becomes.
ST. TERESA OF AVILA

I INTEND TO BE SILENT AND HEAL.

I accept that I have created a lifestyle that distracts me from feeling pain... *I relinquish* fears of becoming still enough that I might feel the pain of separation... *I dream of* Healing... *With peace and love I intend to* return daily to the Stillness within... *I am grateful* to be on the journey Home, *I am.*

Your daily life is your temple
and your religion.
KAHLIL GIBRAN

*R*EFLECTIONS ON OUR OVER CONSUMPTION… So many aspects of our lives are so big. We're big, our cars are big, our homes are big, and our serving sizes are big. Everything seems to be on steroids. 'Super-size me' seems to be the predominant theme of the day. What cost do we pay for everything to be super-sized?

We use more gas for bigger cars and we spend more resources for larger serving sizes of everything from our French fries to our homes to our wardrobes. With so much super-sizing and so much work to pay for it all, our lives have very little 'free' space.

I don't feel like being super-sized anymore. I'm ready to get off the treadmill and relax. I'm ready to rid myself of the large load I am carrying through this life. I want to put it down and take the time to smell the roses.

Instead of super-size me, I choose to maximize me… Maximize being Peaceful and Joyful!

He is a wise man
who does not grieve for the things which he has not,
but rejoices for those which he has.
EPICTETUS

I INTEND TO BE CONTENT.

I accept that some of my desires are rooted in fear and some in Love… *I relinquish* wanting out of fear… *I dream of* slowing down and enjoying life… *With peace and love I intend to* create Beauty… *I am grateful* for the Joy in empty spaces, *I am.*

Gratitude is not only the greatest of virtues,
but the parent of all the others.
CICERO

REFLECTIONS ON ALCHEMY… Last night I woke in the night with thoughts of our strained finances running through my head. I kept thinking and thinking of solutions to our woes and the more I thought the more fearful I became of our dilemma. After probably two hours, I had worked myself into an all out frenzy. Then it occurred to me, "If you want something to be different than what it is, transform it." Stop fighting and accept what is. Relinquish the fears of it. Choose to quiet the mind and listen to the Yearnings of the Heart. Honor the Inspirations by intending them and acting on them. Give thanks. A calm came over me and the sleep that had alluded me just moments before softly enveloped me. In the morning I acted with strength and with Love.

We have the power to transform. As an alchemist works to transform basic metals to precious gold, we have the power to transform our fearful lives into lives of strength that have a foundation of Acceptance, Peace and Love.

Keep transforming your life into something more beautiful. Leave behind fear, anger, judgment and any other negative state and instead choose Love. We too are alchemists in our own right. But we have found something even more desirable than gold. Love.

One who knows more,
loves more.
ST. CATHERINE OF SIENA

I INTEND TO BE LOVING.

I accept the circumstances of my life… *I relinquish* judging people and circumstances to be right or wrong, good or bad… *I dream of* the wisdom to view loveless circumstances as an opportunity to pray for healing… *With peace and love I intend to* honor my heart's yearnings with Intention… *I am grateful* for the Peace and Love that I have found in the pot at the end of the rainbow, *I am.*

ℛEFLECTIONS ON FEMININITY... I feel an urge to honor the feminine by choosing to be feminine. For so many years I've done 'masculine' and felt successful in so many ways. Feminine felt weak to me. Masculine felt independent and strong.

There was an error in my ways. I was labeling one aspect of humanity to be more valuable than another. There is so much beauty in femininity. I want to embrace being a woman and being feminine. I want to cherish being Compassionate, Creative, Graceful and Kind...

I INTEND TO HONOR MY INHERENT NATURE.

I accept that so many of us have forgotten the strength of femininity... *I relinquish* judgment of feminine and masculine traits.... *I dream of* honoring the complimentary forces that create Beauty in our world... *With peace and love I intend to* be comfortable being an expression of my inherent nature... *I am grateful* to be free to be me, *I am.*

*R*EFLECTIONS ON THE POWER TO CHOOSE… Have you ever seen the signs that they sell in the home decorating stores that are printed with quotes? If I were to write a quote to be printed on a sign, it would read 'Live Beautifully.' 'Life is Good' is a great sign, but we could choose to disagree based on our judgment of our current circumstances.

'Live Beautifully' presents us with a choice for how we will choose to be and what we will choose to create. Will we choose to focus our attention on controlling our lives out of fear or will we choose to honor Inspiration and create our lives with Love?

For so long I have tried to control the darkness out of fear. In fighting it I have chosen to focus on it and therefore I find myself standing amidst the dark. I'm ready to let go of trying to control the darkness and instead to focus on living in the Light. I'm ready to choose with Intent.

I am powerful. I can choose with strength. Control is weak. It is done out of fear. I leave behind controlling my life out of fear. I choose power. I choose to honor Inspirations. I choose the Truth of creating my life with Love. I choose to allow the Light within me to burn so brightly that its glow will have beautiful affects. With strength and power I will choose. I will take responsibility for my life and its effects on our world and choose to take another step on the Live Beautifully Journey.

I INTEND TO KNOW HOW POWERFUL I REALLY AM.

I accept that I have free will, the power to choose… *I relinquish* fears of darkness… *I dream of* Living Beautifully… *With peace and love I intend to* take responsibility for creating a beautiful life… *I am grateful* to be aware of my choice to be Creative, *I am.*

*R*EFLECTIONS ON THE GIFT OF GUIDANCE... When you touch a hot stove it is painful. It is a perfect system of Guidance. What hurts has the potential to harm you. On the contrary, what nourishes you feels wonderful. Our emotions are an aspect of our Guidance system. Our feelings are awareness of the emotions, the Guidance.

When we Love it feels 'good.' When we fear it feels 'bad.'

In actuality, there is no opposite to Truth and Love. But there is a way that we cease to be aware of Truth. When we put faith in fearful thoughts, we feel cut off from Truth, from Love, and it hurts like hell. We then experience fearful emotions. That pain, that suffering, is Guidance that what we are doing is harming ourselves. The pain is Guidance to come back to Love, but we tend to not see it that way.

When we suffer we need to look for the thoughts that gave us the illusion of separation; fear in its many forms. Awareness is our first step to taking our hand off of the hot stove and healing.

So many of us haven't known that feeling 'bad' was loving guidance warning us that we were going the wrong way. Because we weren't taught what to do with our feelings, so many of us have just chosen to close ourselves off from them. And thus we find ourselves overcome by the buildup of energies that have gone unrecognized. We carry a load of old painful energy. We carry a load of fear.

The conscience of children is formed by the influences that surround them;
their notions of good and evil
are the result of the moral atmosphere they breathe.
JEAN PAUL RICHTER

I INTEND TO HONOR GUIDANCE.

I accept that we are given Guidance when we Love and when we have strayed from Love... *I relinquish* believing that suffering is bad... *I dream of* accepting the suffering as Guidance to return to Love... *With peace and love I intend to* pay attention to what I am experiencing and I will heed the Guidance and return to Love... *I am grateful* that I am never alone, *I am.*

We choose our joys and sorrows
long before we experience them.
KAHLIL GIBRAN

*R*EFLECTIONS ON A SUBTLE BUT PROFOUND SHIFT... Have you ever seen one of those black and white pictures that can be a completely different drawing depending on how you focus on it? Like the one of a woman. Is she old and ugly or is she young and beautiful? Both exist within the same drawing. What you see depends on your focus. An initial glance and you may see a haggard old woman, but if you keep looking at the picture and adjust your focus just a tiny bit, the picture before you instantly changes and a beautiful young woman appears.

So it is with our lives. People that are accepting and grateful for all that is experience the Light. People that fear their reality and pity themselves experience the illusion of a dark side.

What we see
depends mainly on what we look for.
JOHN LUBBOCK

I INTEND TO SHIFT MY FOCUS.

I accept that I have the choice to focus on my glass as half empty or half full... *I relinquish* judgment of the half that appears to be empty... *I dream of* having Awareness of my free will... *With peace and love I intend to* gently correct myself over and over again... *I am grateful* for the openness that is ready to be filled with wonderful expanding possibilities, *I am.*

A man is not where he lives,
but where he loves.
LATIN PROVERB

*R*EFLECTIONS ON GLIMMERS OF LIGHT... Wouldn't it be wonderful to stand on the moon and observe the earth? I imagine I could see sparks of awakening scattered all over the world. Glimmers here and there as we are experiencing brief moments of awakening. Sparks created by tiny explosions of energy as the love bursts from the confines of our hearts.

From my distant vantage point I would smile as the sparkles intensified in their magnitude and frequency. A sparkle in a location would set off a flurry of more twinkles. More and more sparks. Soon the earth would look as beautiful as a Christmas tree shimmering in exquisite points of Light.

Someday
perhaps the inner light will shine forth from us,
and then
we'll need no other light.
JOHANN WOLFGANG VON GOETHE

I INTEND TO DELIGHT IN THE SPARKLES.

I accept that my life holds no greater opportunity than to awaken and shine... *I relinquish* fears of needing to do anything else... *I dream of* nurturing the spark... *With peace and love I intend to* pass the torch... *I am grateful* for our awakening, *I am.*

When someone steals another's clothes,
we call them a thief.
Should we not give the same name
to one who could clothe the naked and does not?
The bread in your cupboard belongs to the hungry;
the coat unused in your closet belongs to the one who needs it;
the shoes rotting in your closet belong to the one who has no shoes;
the money which you hoard up belongs to the poor.
BASIL THE GREAT

*R*EFLECTIONS ON MY CLOSET... I've been traveling for almost two weeks now with just a small carry-on piece of luggage in tow. When I was packing for this trip I thought that I would feel restrained by my lack of options of what to wear, but instead I find myself feeling free. I don't feel weighed down by my jam-packed closet. I don't feel the need to shop for anything new as I don't have the space to carry it anyway. This too is freeing. It frees me of the stress of having to afford more.

I'm looking forward to going home and sharing my abundance of clothing with someone who needs it. I'm looking forward to a closet that is a reflection of me. Simple, but beautiful, a few choices that are appropriate for the occasions of my life. I'm looking forward to not being weighed down by too much of everything. Simplicity, oh the joy of it!

Simplicity is the ultimate sophistication.
LEONARDO DA VINCI

I INTEND TO LIVE FREELY.

I accept all that I have accumulated... *I relinquish* fears of being wasteful if I let go of something that I paid money for... *I dream of* being free of excessive wanting and having... *With peace and love I intend to* joyfully pass things on to people who can use them... *I am grateful* for being Graceful, *I am.*

*R*EFLECTIONS ON CLEARING A SPACE... I'm ready to let go of the excess things in my life. This accumulation of things has slowly added obligations to my life until there is little space in which to shine.

My life seems to be a continuous juggle of affording and maintaining the stuff. Parting with the stuff sometimes feels like a failure. Parting with the stuff feels unfair as I worked so hard to get it in the first place. But deeper than those feelings is a desire to be free, to be joyful and a casting off of the weight of my responsibilities seems to be the means to accomplish my much desired end.

My husband is frazzled. I yearn to see the playful man he once was prior to taking on so much responsibility. I want freedom. I want to feel free to dance with Joy over the beauty of the dew on the grass. I want to feel free to enjoy the awesome beauty of a sunset.

Just as the birds don't toil 24/7, so too do I want to spend a portion of my day perched outside soaking in the glorious rays of the sun.

The best of life is free to those of us that aren't busy shopping for second-rate stuff in the fluorescent-lit stores.

I INTEND TO CHOOSE TO PERCH IN THE SUN.

I accept the life I've created... *I relinquish* fears of making changes... *I dream of* clearing a space... *With peace and love I intend to* Live Beautifully... *I am grateful* for the courage to change, *I am.*

Through return to simple living comes control of desires.
In control of desires Stillness is attained.
In stillness the world is restored.
LAOZI

*R*EFLECTIONS ON CONNECTING WITH WHAT IS REAL... I'm nearing the end of my vacation and my thoughts are beginning to return to home. I'm a little surprised at what I miss most, solitude and routine. My days lack the moments of solitude and reflection that connect me with what is real.

Wherever I find myself, I plan to fiercely defend my moments of silence, my moments of Stillness. I will create the space for this oh so necessary part of my life. I wonder if someday it will not just be a part of my life, but my way of life?

Lately I find myself exhausted at the end of the day. Within moments of laying horizontal, sleep comes over me. My prayers of gratitude for the day are cut short by sleep.

A new pattern is emerging. I find myself waking in the night and enjoying an hour or so of prayer and reflection before drifting back to sleep. I find myself enjoying the tranquil Stillness of the dark night. There is so much beauty in the Stillness.

I have never found a companion
that was so companionable as solitude.
HENRY DAVID THOREAU

I INTEND TO SEEK STILLNESS.

I accept that I have chosen a frenzied lifestyle... *I relinquish* fears of missing out on anything... *I dream of* having the wisdom to choose moments of Stillness at the beginning and end of every day... *With peace and love I intend to* honor my choice to Live Beautifully... *I am grateful* to be Aware of my choices, *I am.*

It is only possible to live happily ever after on a day-to-day basis.
MARGARET WANDER BONNANO

*R*EFLECTIONS ON OUR CASTLES... We devote such a large portion of our lives earning money and then spending it on a bunch of stuff. We have another option. If we chose to buy less stuff, we could work less and spend that time tending to ourselves.

It's like we've been on a treadmill that has an automatic speed increaser and it's going so fast we're fearful of the impact if we were to try jumping off. We're working like crazy to keep up with our frantic lives. We see the serene photographs of beautiful tranquil people and think, "Wow, what I wouldn't do for a slice of that life!" But so many of us wake up the next day and do what we despise all over again.

Let's start seeing the choices we make in our day. When faced with a choice of how we will spend our precious commodity called time, pause and listen to that little voice inside. Are we tired of running? Running home, running to work, running to get the kids, running errands... (What is it we're chasing anyway?)

Do we have what we really want already? Do we just need to stop for a moment and do what we really want to do? Are we stuck on the 'having'? Do we yearn to focus on 'being'? Are we so caught up in lower realm wanting that we have little time to honor our soulful yearnings?

As we walk through our day let's see the opportunities for choice. Choose well dear friends, let's reign over our kingdoms with grace and dignity. Let's do more than just furnish our castles. Let's choose to Live Beautifully in our kingdoms.

If you were renewed by grace,
and were to meet your old self,
I am sure you would be very anxious to get out of his company.
CHARLES H. SPURGEON

I AM GRATEFUL TO HONOR MY YEARNINGS FOR GRACE AND DIGNITY.

I accept that I am plagued with an addiction to more... *I relinquish* feeding this addiction... *I dream of* being free from lower realm wantings... *With peace and love I intend to* be aware of desires that are aligned with Truth and Love and desires that are merely an attempt to satisfy a craving for more... *I am grateful* to be free from the darkness that creates unhealthy thinking and cravings, *I am.*

Reflect upon your present blessings,
of which every man has many,
not on your past misfortunes,
of which all men have some.
CHARLES DICKENS

*R*EFLECTIONS ON GETTING OFF TO A GOOD START… Just as I am the type of person that slowly walks into a body of water, gently letting my body adapt to its new surroundings, so are my days. I choose to rise early enough to allow myself to gently ease into the day.

Settled into my comfy chair, I light a candle, gaze at the sunrise, a hot cup of coffee in my hand… I begin my day with thanks, with prayers of gratitude. I begin my day relinquishing the fears of the day and asking for Grace to flow through me. I sit in the Stillness that allows me to sense the grandness of the creation than I am a part of.

Some days I rise from my chair and do a little Tai Chi in the sunlight. A graceful moving meditation that slowly and gently wakes my body.

Without my morning meditation my day can be frazzled. I lack the focus to accomplish all that is set before me. I get through my tasks with sheer determination instead of a flow of Grace. It's like I have to take the time to establish a Connection or I find myself running out of energy half way through the day.

Beauty without grace
is the hook without the bait.
RALPH WALDO EMERSON

I INTEND TO CONNECT EACH AND EVERY DAY.

I accept that some activities are not optional: brushing my teeth, showering, eating, prayer, meditation, & reflection to name a few… *I relinquish* fears of not having time in my day to tend to myself… *I dream of* having the discipline to care for myself... *With peace and love I intend to* honor my daily devotion... *I am grateful* for the effects of Grace in our world, *I am.*

*R*EFLECTIONS ON FOLLOWING YOUR BLISS… So why is it that by 'following your bliss' we tend to enjoy success? Does bliss refer to doing what you love? Are bliss and love our experience when we live with Truth? Does doing what you love refer to doing exactly what you were created to do? What comes naturally to you? Is bliss our emotion when we are creating with Love? Does it mean completely losing ourselves in an activity? i.e. losing not our true self, but enjoying the bliss of freedom from the lower realm?

When we are in that moment of bliss, free from all of the yitziness of the lower realm blockages, are we inclined to be open to Inspiration? Is Grace able to freely flow through us and into our tasks?

Why is it that the most 'successful' people are 'in touch'? 'In touch' with what? Does it mean that when you pursue your passion that you are honoring your inherent nature, living and creating with Love?

*He who has overcome his fears
will truly be free.*
ARISTOTLE

I INTEND TO PURSUE BLISS.

I accept that some parts of my life just don't fit… *I relinquish* fears of letting go of old ways… *I dream of* having the wisdom to do what I love… *With peace and love I intend to* Live Beautifully as I uniquely define it… *I am grateful* for the Joy of being authentically me, *I am.*

~ 130 ~

*R*EFLECTIONS ON FEELING DISPLACED... When I was a little girl, as far back as I can remember, I had this steady feeling of uneasiness. I felt like I was in the wrong place. At the time I felt very alone in my suffering.

Instead of feeling as though I was in the wrong place, was I just feeling separate? The same sense of separateness that so much of humanity feels?

I likened it to physically being in the wrong place. But instead of being physically in the wrong place, was I just sensing the lessening of my Trueness as the lower realm patterns grew and strengthened? Was I sensing the lessening of an Upper Realm existence as I experienced lower realm situations and based my developing belief system on this falseness?

Had I known it once, did I slumber in my crib blissful in the sense of my Oneness with All? As the falseness grew within me creating a sense of separation, is that what made me feel like I was in the wrong place? Is that what created the insatiable hunger to seek? Did I want to get back to what I had once known?

Unity is vision;
it must have been part of the process of learning to see.
HENRY ADAMS

I INTEND TO BECOME AWARE OF A FALSE SENSE OF SEPARATION.

I accept my feelings of separation from both Heaven and Earth... *I relinquish* fears of being alone... *I dream of* the veil being lifted that obscures my vision of my Oneness with All... *With peace and love I intend to* embrace the knowing that I was born in the perfect place, at the perfect time, perfectly me... *I am grateful* to remember, *I am.*

$\mathcal{R}$EFLECTIONS ON LABELING... I realize that I have labeled objects in my life. I realize that I have perceived objects to carry a 'weight,' depending on their monetary cost. Things that are expensive carry a different perception than things that are not expensive.

A full-price $50 pillow has a different 'feel' than the same pillow on a bottom-dollar sale. In reality they can essentially be the same pillow, it is just in my mental labeling that they become different in my mind.

I want to perceive things for simply what they are, beautiful expressions of creativity. No price tags attached. No feelings of ownership attached. Just things that are.

A gorgeous sunset is easy to experience without labels. No one owns it. No label of being mine or yours. No one paid for it last night as the financial sponsor of the great event. No label of having a monetary value. You don't have to buy a ticket for it as an exclusive event for the rich and famous. It just is. Period. Without the labeling our experience of it can be Joyful.

I want to enjoy all of creation in that way. Just aspects of creation that are there for the sake of Joy.

I INTEND TO BE AWARE OF JUDGMENT.

I accept the falseness of believing that my worthiness can be enhanced by having expensive things... *I relinquish* judging things... *I dream of* a change in my perception... *With peace and love I intend to* enjoy beauty for the sake of Joy... *I am grateful* for a shift in my perception, *I am.*

Don't rely too much on labels,
For too often they are fables.
CHARLES H. SPURGEON

$\mathcal{R}$EFLECTIONS ON MORE LABELING... I'm realizing that I label activities in my day as well. An hour spent on an activity that earns my income has a different label than an hour spent at home doing laundry. I can spend a morning caring for my home and feel like I haven't accomplished a thing because the activities I engaged in didn't earn money.

I label activities differently when really they are all just activities. I judge them and put them into a hierarchy of worthiness.

I will drop the judgment and just go about the activities of my day. Honoring every moment for the gift that it is.

I never approve,
or disapprove,
of anything now.
It is an absurd attitude to take towards life.
OSCAR WILDE

I INTEND TO BE AWARE OF JUDGMENT.

I accept that I have labeled activities... *I relinquish* the need to control, the need for approval and the need to judge… *I dream of* seeing things with knowing eyes... *With peace and love I intend to* honor every moment with gratitude... *I am grateful* for awareness of the lower realm, *I am.*

If you are alone you belong entirely to yourself.
If you are accompanied by even one companion
you belong only half to yourself
or even less in proportion to the thoughtlessness of his conduct
and if you have more than one companion
you will fall more deeply into the same plight.
LEONARDO DA VINCI

*R*EFLECTIONS ON COMA VISION... As a people we generally choose to zone out when we feel the desire to escape the stresses of the day. We sit back, turn on the tube and enter what grandpa used to call 'coma vision.'

We've got it wrong. To recharge our batteries we need to zone in, not zone out. We need to turn off our frantic brains so that we can zone in, be aware of our Essence. We become 'out of touch' when we live in a manner of constant external stimulation which sometimes seems like a better alternative to distract us from the incessant thinking of our crazy brains.

I want to turn it all off. The voice in my head and the noisy chatter of a TV. Once I've cleared the slate so to speak, then I want to turn it on again, but in a different way.

Nowhere can man find a quieter
or more untroubled retreat
than in his own soul.
MARCUS AURELIUS

I INTEND TO ZONE IN, NOT OUT.

I accept that I create distractions in an effort to relax... *I relinquish* fears of Stillness and Silence... *I dream of* having the capacity to see the things I use to dull my feelings, my awareness of emotions... *With peace and love I intend to* learn to quiet myself... *I am grateful* for the courage to be aware, *I am.*

*R*EFLECTIONS ON NATURE… So what belongs to the 'natural world'? What is a part of nature? What isn't natural? How do we distinguish parts of creation to be natural and other parts to be unnatural? The false beliefs in separation are the source of this judgment.

I am a beautiful aspect of a beautiful creation. There is no natural and unnatural. Anything that feels unnatural is just something that I am judging, including my mental concept of me.

With the diminishment of judgment comes a wonderful Awareness of the Unity of all of Creation. With the diminishment of judgment the sense of separation falls away and an unbridled Joy fill the space as the truth of the Oneness with All is revealed.

I wonder if the snow loves the trees and fields,
that it kisses them so gently?
And then it covers them up snug, you know,
with a white quilt;
and perhaps it says
"Go to sleep, darlings,
till the summer comes again."
LEWIS CARROLL

I INTEND TO SENSE THE ONENESS OF ALL.

I accept that I have believed that there was separation… *I relinquish* believing everything that I was taught… *I dream of* being aware when I think thoughts of judgment and experience the emotions that come from the false need for control, approval and judgment… *With peace and love I intend to* know of the Oneness of All… *I am grateful* for moments of Clarity, *I am.*

$\mathcal{R}$EFLECTIONS ON ADVICE FROM A FRIEND... Many years ago a friend gave me some great advice, but I didn't understand it at the time.

My family had been treated very poorly by people we loved dearly. When I saw my friend I was overcome with sobs and sorrow. I spewed out to him in detail the horrible situation of how we had been wronged and how we were suffering.

He looked at me with strength and said, "Stop it!! Let it go. Just let it go! Stop brain ____ing yourself!"

I see that when I replay the scenario of being wronged over and over again, I feel more and more disconnected and the suffering grows.

When this happens I need to stop. I need to become aware when circumstances trigger fearful beliefs and emotions. I need to be aware of the story that my mind keeps replaying. I need to see the insanity. I need to let it go. I need to find an Upper Realm thought. I need to find an Upper Realm choice of action. I need to choose instead to be a beautiful expression of creation unencumbered by the ugliness of an accumulation of old false thought and emotions.

I INTEND TO BE AWARE WHEN FALSENESS IS TRIGGERED.

I accept that I am not alone in my habit of dwelling on what happened in the past... *I relinquish* the habit of feeding the old pain the fearful emotions that it craves... *I dream of* being free of the kharmic debt from my errors of the past... *With peace and love I intend to* ask for the healing of my mind of the falseness that I have based my past errors on and then I will ask for forgiveness... *I am grateful* for Forgiveness, the undoing of the consequences of my errors, the times when I missed the mark of Love, *I am.*

The world is but a canvas to the imagination.
HENRY DAVID THOREAU

EFLECTIONS ON CREATING A GARDEN... Some aspects of my life are weak. They lack the robust vitality of other aspects of my life. Each day I will tend to the weaknesses by seeking them out and tending to them.

Each morning as I journal, I will relinquish the fears and then I will sow the seeds of Abundance and Vitality. I will record in my journal thoughts of Abundance, Peace, Love, Prosperity and Vitality. I will nourish these seeds by reveling in my optimistic beliefs and my faithful spirit.

I will not just celebrate the aspects of my life that are energetic and well, but I will tend to the aspects that are weak and in need of growth. Acceptance, Peace, Love and Joy, these are the powerful forces of energy that bring life to the seeds in our Gardens of Eden.

The greater part of our happiness
or misery
depends upon our disposition,
not upon our circumstances.
MARTHA WASHINGTON

I INTEND TO CREATE BEAUTY.

I accept myself as I am... *I relinquish* fears of my shadows... *I dream of* creating a beautiful life... *With peace and love I intend to* honor my dreams as seeds of potential... *I am grateful* for my capacity to create with Love, *I am.*

Recovering our health and then learning to create health on a daily basis
involves naming our experiences for what they are
—no matter how painful—
and then learning that the motor for our lives is with us,
regardless of our past.
CHRISTIANE NORTHRUP, M.D.

*R*EFLECTIONS ON A CLEAN ABODE... An important step to gaining health is to give a name to your illness. It is a necessary step to regaining wellness.

So it is with the illness of our minds. Our lower realm thought patterns come in so many disguises. It is essential to become Aware of them and name them before it is possible to rid ourselves of the effects of them.

Just as a homemaker relentlessly cleans every inch of her home in the springtime, scrubbing and scouring on hands and knees looking with a keen eye for the dirt that has accumulated through the long winter, so should be the cleaning of our Beings. To be powerful creators we need clarity: mind, body and spirit. Let's devote ourselves to a daily task of searching and identifying our fears, worries, judgments and needs for approval. Let's use the "I relinquish" step within the journaling to name our illnesses and rid ourselves of them. As we eliminate one lower realm thought pattern after another, we will be cleansing ourselves so that we are able to Live Beautifully. Cast them out just as you would shake the dust from a beautiful rug, snapping it in the sunshine and watching the dust float through the air.

Roll up your sleeves and get to the task of cleaning. When we're finished we will be bright and anew. Once our dwellings are clean we will stand ready to chase out the dirt that may attempt to creep back into our tidy abodes.

One, who maintains cleanliness keeps away diseases.
THE SAM VEDA

I INTEND TO BE PURE.

I *accept* the daily task of cleaning my abode... *I relinquish* fears of facing the dirt... *I dream of* having eyes that see the grains of sand that irritate me... *With peace and love I intend to* seek out that which obscures the beautiful me and release it to the wind... *I am grateful* for my daily cleansing, *I am.*

Just as a snake sheds its skin,
we must shed our past over and over again.
BUDDHA

REFLECTIONS ON WHAT WE'RE WORTHY OF... Last night we watched the movie *Maid in Manhattan*. Jennifer Lopez plays the part of a maid who dreams of more for her life but runs into mental blocks as she doesn't believe that she is worthy of 'more.' She has all of the characteristics needed for her desires but she can't seem to shake her mother's voice in her head to not expect too much and to play it safe. Merissa has heard her mother's words so many times that she struggles to get them out of her head. They keep her in a pattern of living in fear and doubt.

In a moment of intense emotions and recognition she explodes at her mother and commands that she stop. This is a turning point as she becomes Aware of her thinking and thus begins the transition from living her life in fear, to living her life with Love.

I recognize this pattern in myself and my own family. My grandma and my parents mean well, but they have passed some of their fears on to me. I too have done the same with my own children. I am going to recognize this destructive behavior when it happens in the future and give it a resounding 'STOP' with an outstretched hand in the face. Not an act of violence, but an act of warding off the fearful thought patterns. I will cleanse myself of thoughts of unworthiness and cease to pass these on to the next generation. I will be a Cinderella. With dreams of a beautiful life I will cast off the rags and the drudgery. With thoughts of my dreams and an infusion of beautiful Light, I will magically transform into the beautiful princess that is my Truth.

What we are today comes from our thoughts of yesterday,
and our present thoughts build our life of tomorrow:
Our life is the creation of our mind.
BUDDHA

I INTEND TO KNOW THAT I AM WORTHY OF A BEAUTIFUL LIFE.

I accept that I have felt unworthy... *I relinquish* fears of needing to play it safe and not expect too much... *I dream of* pursuing my inspirations with confidence... *With peace and love I intend to* transform my thinking... *I am grateful* to know that I have the capacity to create a beautiful life, *I am.*

$\mathcal{R}$EFLECTIONS ON CHANGING OUR MINDS... You can never think your way to peacefulness. You can only 'be' peaceful. If peace is your pursuit, learn to be. What does it mean to 'be'? It means to live from a state of Awareness. It means to live without a mind full of repetitive thought. It means to live without a head that is full of fearful thinking that leads to a state of being that is anxious and tense. Becoming aware of our mind is our ticket to living in a state of serenity.

Become aware of your thoughts. Watch what happens. Observe how fearful thoughts create tension in your body. Acknowledge what results from your fearful thinking; a hindrance of the flow of Love and Light.

Keep observing your thinking. Feel gratitude. Choose to accept things as they are. Choose to relinquish the fears. Choose to quiet the mind. Accept a new way of being. Accept a new way of thinking; inspired thinking that comes from a place of Acceptance and Love, not from a place of fear. Those inspired thoughts will manifest in emotions and actions that will be a reflection of Light and Love.

*The aim of Life is to Live,
and to Live means to be Aware,
joyously,
drunkenly,
serenely,
divinely,
Aware.*
HENRY JAMES

I INTEND TO BE AWARE OF OUR THINKING.

I accept that my mind is seldom still... *I relinquish* fearful and pointless thinking... *I dream of* quieting my restless mind so that I can hear the Inspired Thoughts... *With peace and love I intend to* be Aware of the doubts and fears that follow the Inspired Thoughts... *I am grateful* for growing Awareness, *I am*.

Loss is nothing else but change,
and change is nature's delight.
MARCUS AURELIUS

*R*EFLECTIONS ON RESISTANCE... Last night was bad. I was down and out. I wanted the moment to be over. I was heavily resisting what was. My body responded with my back going out of alignment. Pain and fatigue were my reality. I wished to run away from my life and return to my vacation where I had so much energy and my body was true. I pondered the circumstances of my life that yearned for change, for growth.

This morning I realize that it isn't my circumstances, but my state of being, my spirit that needs altering. On vacation I took the experience as it came. I had very few plans. I walked softly and experienced with acceptance whatever came my way. I felt calm, soft and gentle.

Life always seems to give you the experiences you need for growth. I guess I need to work on being Aware of what I perceive as adversities. Just when you get comfortable, life demands that you step out of your comfort zone and grow a little more.

The universe is change;
our life is what our thoughts make it.
MARCUS AURELIUS

I INTEND TO BE PEACEFUL.

I accept that growing can be painful if you resist it... *I relinquish* fears of circumstances that seem to be wrong... *I dream of* knowing that my pain is a Nudge to move, to change, to grow, to evolve... *With peace and love I intend to* surrender another layer of falseness that justifies controlling out of fear and instead embrace the choice of creating with Love... *I am grateful* that Life keeps giving me the perfect circumstances for the evolution of my soul, *I am.*

Don't loaf and invite inspiration;
light out after it with a club.
JACK LONDON

*R*EFLECTIONS ON THE NUDGES… Life nudges me in the direction of the Flow. The Nudges are little Inspirations that creep in, i.e., an idea that pops into my head from out of the Blue. Life yearns to come forth and blossom. So many attempts to flower and yet the creation is often blocked. Blocked by my thoughts, my fears, my doubts. How many times have I received an Inspiration and then the excitement that comes with it like fuel for its take off only to be thwarted by my thinking? The lower realm thoughts creep in and say to me "Well that sounds so fine, but___, but____, but____… " and I'm convinced not to follow the Inspiration but remain safe and tight in the bud.

I intend to honor the Guidance. I intend to recognize it as Creation attempting to come through me. The Nudges are like a knock on the door. I intend to recognize the Knocks. I intend to open the door.

I intend to be an opening for Creation to bloom. I intend to recognize that fear blocks the flow of Inspiration, the flow of Creation.

Genius is one percent inspiration,
ninety-nine percent perspiration.
THOMAS EDISON

I INTEND TO SAY 'YES' TO GUIDANCE.

I accept that Creation attempts to express itself through us… *I relinquish* the fears that block it… *I dream of* being an opening for Creation… *With peace and love I intend to* be attentive to the Yearnings, the Nudges… *I am grateful* for the opportunity to bloom, *I am.*

Let yourself be silently drawn
by the strange pull of what you really love.
It will not lead you astray.
RUMI

*R*EFLECTIONS ON YEARNINGS... Wanting... Yearning... What's the difference between wanting and Yearning? Wanting seems to come from a place of control. Yearning seems to be a state of surrender to that which pulls me in the direction that Life desires to unfold. I will become creative by honoring the Yearnings.

The best antidote I have found is to yearn for something.
As long as you yearn, you can't congeal:
there is a forward motion to yearning.
GAIL GODWIN

I INTEND TO HONOR MY YEARNINGS.

I accept that I am repulsed and drawn by forces... *I relinquish* fears of needing to think through and rationalize everything... *I dream of* living my life perceiving Guidance... *With peace and love I intend to* honor that which pulls on my heart... *I am grateful* for awareness of soulful Yearnings and lower realm wantings, *I am.*

If we admit that we are in the stream of evolution,
then each circumstance must be to us quite right.
HELENA BLAVATSKY

*R*EFLECTIONS ON A GENTLE UNFOLDING... Yearnings feel like pulls to me, Nudges feel like pushes. Both feel like gentle Guidance that is offered. Yesterday I honored the Guidance and my day unfolded beautifully. A thought popped in my head to call my sister. I was on a bike ride and thought it better to wait until I was home. But remembering my choice to honor the Nudges I called. I few minutes into the conversation she shared that my call came at the perfect moment. She really needed someone to talk to. I wonder if lots of people felt or had a thought to call her when she needed someone to reach out at that difficult time. When one of us needs is there an opposing desire to give? Is there lack in this world due to our not responding to Nudges because our action is negated by lower realm thinking?

It reminds me of a wallet that a dear friend made for me. Each that she makes has a few choice words on its cover that she chooses just for you. Mine says 'Unplan Your Life.' I found it interesting that she would choose that for me. The words seem to offer so much wisdom for me. I've been a Type A list-making highly-functional woman. The problem with being overly organized is that you don't have the flexibility to step into the Flow and allow your life to gently unfold. When every moment is preplanned it takes away your spontaneity. There's no room for synchronicity. It's difficult to sense the Yearnings and the Nudges. If I choose to unplan my life, I can open up to life coming through me instead of always following the pre-made plan outfitted with a safety net.

Why not seize the pleasure at once?
How often is happiness destroyed by preparation,
foolish preparation!
JANE AUSTEN

I INTEND TO SURRENDER TO THE FLOW OF LIFE.

I accept that life can be a gentle unfolding... *I relinquish* expectations that lead me to wanting to have a plan... *I dream of* perceiving the Nudges... *With peace and love I intend to* honor Creation by responding to Guidance... *I am grateful* for the beautiful Flow that waits for me to step into it, *I am.*

REFLECTIONS ON MY MORNING RITUAL... Some mornings I engage in a creative endeavor. I sit cross legged with a candle burning, a blanket in my lap, coffee in hand and I breathe. I dream. And I dream some more.

It is like a creative brain storming session. I sit with a journal and pen and write. This is where I sit quiet enough to listen to the Life that yearns to come forth.

I listen to the Yearnings and write them down. This is where they transform from a wispy breeze, a fleeting thought, to something denser, words on a page. I roll them around in my mind and they become larger and stronger. The energy strengthens as it quickens and readies to manifest in our world.

Dreams are like seeds just waiting for the opportunity to sprout and grow. So many begin their growth but are ended before their full potential by that which stunts so much of Life, fearful thinking.

I intend for my life to be a flourishing garden. And so I will return each morning to see what comes and choose to strengthen the possibilities with Love rather than stunt them with fear. I intend to create a Garden of Eden wherever I may be, a place where Life can flourish free of judgment and fearful expectation.

To see things in the seed,
that is genius.
LAOZI

I INTEND TO BE CREATIVE.

I accept that Life yearns to come through us... *I relinquish* fears that block creation... *I dream of* Healing... *I dream of* a spacious life that allows for Creativity... *With peace and love I intend to* honor Inspired thoughts... *I am grateful* for the Love that flows when Heaven meets Earth, *I am.*

If you want to find God,
hang out in the space between your thoughts.
ALAN COHEN

*R*EFLECTIONS ON THE DENSITY WITHIN ME... When I meditate in the morning I close my eyes. I gently dismiss my thoughts until my mind rests and I am able to enter the Stillness where I am aware of myself without thinking of myself. The Awareness within me observes the energies of my body; energies that are Light and Vibrant and others that are dark and dense.

With Awareness the energies sometimes strengthen, sometimes lessen, sometimes move.

Most days my pelvic region is dense. My heart is open and bright. Sometimes a denseness will travel up my body until it is in my throat area and I find myself opening my mouth to allow its continued movement as it leaves me. Some days my body is alive with so much energy, other days it is not.

Love is a vital energy. Fear blocks the flow of Love. Keep relinquishing the fears and in doing so you strengthen the flow of Peace and Love. In doing so, you will be a creator of the good stuff. You will be a creator of a new world. You will be choosing to Live Beautifully.

I must choose between despair and Energy—
I choose the latter.
JOHN KEATS

I INTEND TO BE AWARE OF THE FLOW OF ENERGIES.

I accept that there are places within me where Love is blocked from flowing... *I relinquish* fears of opening up old pain... *I dream of* being aware of the blockages created by accumulations of dark energies... *With peace and love I intend to* be gentle and compassionate as I accept the Light that dissipates the darkness; Awareness followed by Compassion instead of Awareness followed by judgment... *I am grateful* for the healing affects of Light, *I am.*

Sewing mends the soul.
UNKNOWN

REFLECTIONS ON MY STITCHING... I feel different the last few days. The days are getting shorter and the air is cooler and crisper. With the changes in the weather come changes in me. I'm ready to return to my embroidery project; a fabulous cocky rooster in bright bold colors on black fabric.

Stitching doesn't just result in a pretty something to hang upon my wall. It gives me hours of meditative bliss. When I stitch my mind focuses on the task before me, on the feel of the strands of wool, the beautiful colors, the sound of the thread passing through the fabric, the placement of the next stitch.

The frantic mind relaxes in the trance of the repetitive strokes of the hand. Push. Pull. Push. Pull. The opposing forces are relaxing. Like walking or riding a bike.

I love sitting with my daughter when she knits. Her body sits so gracefully and relaxed while her fingers seem to fly so effortlessly. So much action within a state of calm.

A cluttered mind is challenged to hold its own when I engage in a creative pleasure. As I slip into my creative bliss, the clutter in my mind slowly recedes and fades away.

Methinks it is a token of healthy and gentle characteristics,
when women of high thoughts and accomplishments love to sew;
especially as they are never more at home with their own hearts
than while so occupied.
NATHANIEL HAWTHORNE

I INTEND TO MEND MY SOUL.

I accept that watching television has largely replaced the time for creativity in our society...
I relinquish believing in false thoughts of the lack of time in my day for creative pleasures...
I dream of creating with my hands... *With peace and love I intend to* honor my Yearnings to create something beautiful... *I am grateful* to be creative, *I am.*

However mean your life is,
meet it and live it.
HENRY DAVID THOREAU

REFLECTIONS ON INSOMNIA... I have been waking in the night lately unable to fall back to sleep for an hour or sometimes even more. Has caffeine too late in the day been the culprit? No. Unfortunately it has been darkness that has reared its ugly head. There has been so much crap in my life in the last month, surely I am justified in not being accepting of what is. Surely there is justification in lying in bed at night uptight and worried over the circumstances of the day.

I am miserable. I yearn for Peace. Will I only find peace in the idyllic days or will I learn to stop judging circumstances as good or bad, right or wrong and just accept life exactly as it is?

Is a day at the beach any more right or good than a day of 'troubles' that resulted in learning to return to Love?

I'm done judging what happens. Life just is. No matter what happens. Peace be with you, Doris. Every day.

Everything in life that we really accept
undergoes a change.
KATHERINE MANSFIELD

I INTEND TO ACCEPT LIFE AS IT IS.

I accept that the experiences in my life are perfect for the evolution of my soul... *I relinquish* judgment of circumstances that I perceive to be unpleasant... *I dream of* having the wisdom to take life as it comes... *With peace and love I intend* to return to my breath when my mind gets carried away... *I am grateful* to be aware of when I feel justified, *I am.*

Everything is in motion.
Everything flows.
Everything is vibrating.
WILLIAM HAZLITT

$\mathcal{R}$EFLECTIONS ON BEING VIBRANT... I feel a pull to be vibrant. I want to let go of being tense and rigid. I yearn to be a bright flow of loving energy. When I live in this state I seem to feel a vibration within me. Is that where the word vibrant comes from?

When we are vibrant are we free from tenseness created by the energies that we carry? Is the trueness of our being able to shine through in a flow of loving vibrations that emanate from our being?

When someone is glowing is that too a state of being where Life shines through? When we are open to others does that mean we are free from the blockages that form walls around our hearts?

Vibrant, glowing, open... I yearn to be an opening for love to flow into our world.

Let there be light.
GENESIS 1:3

I INTEND TO BE GROUNDED TO LIFE AND OPEN TO LIGHT.

I accept that blockages obscure my connection to Heaven and Earth... *I relinquish* all that blocks Union... *I dream of* the walls coming down... *I dream of* being free from the consequences of my past errors... *With peace and love I intend to* seek awareness of my errors and ask for healing... *I am grateful* for Forgiveness, *I am.*

Order is the sanity of the mind,
the health of the body,
the peace of the city,
the security of the state.
Like beams in a house or bones to a body,
so is order to all things.
ROBERT SOUTHEY

REFLECTIONS ON LIST MAKING... Are you a list maker? I am. I used to think I was a list maker out of some kind of insanity, but now I'm beginning to see it as a tool *for* sanity.

If I have to hold on to information in my head, "pick up so & so, do this, do that..." it prevents my mind from being able to fully relax. By writing things down I can clear a space in my head for open expansiveness knowing that all I need to remember will be there when I'm ready for it.

Forgetfulness is a form of freedom.
KAHLIL GIBRAN

I INTEND TO ENJOY THE BEAUTY OF ORDER.

I accept the long list of requests that are made of me... *I relinquish* fears of saying 'no'... *I relinquish* allowing other peoples' expectations to affect me... *I dream of* having the wisdom to recognize when I say yes because of fears... *With peace and love I intend to* follow the wisdom of my heart... *I am grateful* for Awareness of my free will, *I am*... *I am grateful* for my choice to create what I will, *I am*.

He who has overcome his fears
will truly be free.
ARISTOTLE

*R*EFLECTIONS ON MY MIND... For so long my mind has been something to be reckoned with. It has had a life of its own. Streams of incessant thought have exhausted me. Worries plagued my thinking. The lion is slowly being tamed. The same mind that plagued me is an amazing tool when I'm in charge of using it!

When my mind isn't full, there is so much good to come of it. When it has a life of its own it plagues me. It's like the difference between being an unwilling passenger in a runaway car or being the driver of a Ferrari on a beautiful mountainside road. Oh the thrill of having so much power and so much acceleration, so much performance.

Let's jump out of the runaway cars and find the keys to our Ferraris!

You have power over your mind,
not outside events.
Realize this,
and you will find strength.
MARCUS AURELIUS

I INTEND TO KNOW THE POWER OF MY INTENTIONS.

I accept that fearful thinking disconnects me from our Father... *I relinquish* fears of being alone and out of control... *I dream of* remembering my Oneness with the Power that drives all... *With peace and love I intend to* quiet my mind and be at Peace... *I am grateful* for moments of Serenity, *I am.*

The greatest gift that you can give to others
is the gift of unconditional love and acceptance.
BRIAN TRACY

℞EFLECTIONS ON MAKING UPPER REALM CHOICES... Can you be accepting when the people around you feel insecure or does it bother you? Can you accept their fearful lower realm behaviors or do they inconvenience you? Can you accept the outburst after someone's pain body has been triggered or are you angry that you have to put up with it? Do you respond to darkness with a prayer for Healing or with judgment and resentment?

The wound
is the place where the Light enters you.
RUMI

I INTEND TO MAKE UPPER REALM CHOICES
IN LOWER REALM SITUATIONS.

I accept the stirrings of the lower realm energies in me when faced with it in others... *I relinquish* fears of other people bringing me down... *I dream of* knowing that my perception of darkness is Inspiration to respond with prayers for Healing... *With peace and love I intend to* pray for healing when I witness feelings of unworthiness, doubt, anger, judgment, resentment, discontent, envy, jealousy... *I am grateful* for the change that occurs when I respond with Awareness, Acceptance, Compassion and Prayer, *I am. I am grateful* to be aware of Upper Realm responses to lower realm situations, *I am.*

There is nothing more dreadful than the habit of doubt.
Doubt separates people.
It is a poison that disintegrates friendships
and breaks up pleasant relations.
It is a thorn that irritates and hurts;
it is a sword that kills.
BUDDHA

REFLECTIONS ON DOUBT... So what is it that creates doubt? To doubt we had to have a belief of what was right. Doubt is the uncertainty that comes when there is a stirring within ourselves that loosens the grips of what we have believed to be true.

How many rules have we learned in our lifetime about what we should believe, how we should behave, or how we should look? We are taught so many rules by people who intend to help us to be good. But what happens when someone decides to change a rule? That creates so much uncertainty, so much doubt. Gosh, then we must have been wrong before. Therefore we weren't good. Right or wrong. Good or bad. So many rules to keep us on the right path.

I yearn to evolve. Evolution needs the openness to change. To just be. I yearn to let go of the rules. I yearn to be accepting of how I am in any given moment without a doubt that I am right or wrong, good or bad. I yearn to know that life unfolds, therefore it changes. I desire to let go of the rigidness. I no longer wish to figure out what is right and what is wrong.

Love and doubt have never been on speaking terms.
KAHLIL GIBRAN

I INTEND TO SEE DOUBT AND CHOOSE LOVE.

I accept that humanity has created rules out of fear of being wrong... *I relinquish* doubt and expectation... *I dream of* simply living with Love... *With peace and love I intend to* let judgment fall away... *I am grateful* for awareness of doubt, *I am.*

*R*EFLECTIONS ON THE WINDS OF CHANGE... We are constantly being moved by the 'winds of change.' Put your face to the wind and smile. Dance with it. Soar with it if you feel inclined.

Kites are a beautiful example of dancing with the wind. To achieve great heights they must adjust to the wind with a delicate balance of resistance, flow and groundedness. If they maintain their groundedness, their Connection to our Earthly Mother, they dance in the sky attaining greater and greater height. If they become disconnected, they are sure to crash and burn.

Doubt disconnects us from Love. Love is the energy that grounds us. Entertain doubt, and we cut off the Love. Cut off the Love, and we crash and burn.

Doubt...
is an illness that comes from knowledge
and leads to madness.
GUSTAVE FLAUBERT

I INTEND TO DANCE WITH THE WINDS OF CHANGE.

I accept that I can't fly unless I am grounded... *I relinquish* holding on to judgments of the past... *I dream of* letting go of all that blocks my capacity to be rooted to Creation... *With peace and love I intend to* do the necessary work to create the clarity that is necessary for my growth... *I am grateful* to be grounded, *I am.*

*R*EFLECTIONS ON LISTENING... I want to learn to listen. I want to let go of my regimented lifestyle so that I have the space in my life to listen and respond. To listen to the soft and gentle nudges that I feel, that I sense. To respond with the love that flows from my heart. I want to listen to the inspirations that seem to just come out of the blue. When one of those comes and I respond to it immediately, there is a special flow to life; a beautiful unfolding that feels so blissful.

I yearn to quiet the voice in my head; to live in the Stillness so that when Wisdom speaks I just might hear it.

A wise old owl sat on an oak;
The more he saw the less he spoke;
The less he spoke the more he heard;
Why aren't we like that wise old bird?
AUTHOR UNKNOWN

I INTEND TO LISTEN WITH JOYFUL ANTICIPATION.

I accept that the noise in my head drowns out the Voice that I yearn to hear... *I relinquish* fears of needing to think things through... *I dream of* having the wisdom to choose a quiet gentle existence... *With peace and love I intend to* honor Inspiration by expressing it... *I am grateful* to be in the Flow, *I am.*

Just as a snake sheds its skin,
we must shed our past over and over again.
BUDDHA

*R*EFLECTIONS ON A SLY OLD FOX... Lower realm thinking is a sly old fox. It can creep in and mask itself in the least of obvious ways. After our house was burglarized, staying in the Upper Realm amongst all the hubbub of dealing with police officers, insurance people, my sense of loss, and the reaccumulation of stuff was a challenge. A challenge that I did not do well with. I felt totally justified in being totally immersed in the lower realm: mind, body and spirit.

I was miserable. Amongst all that ick, remembering the Truth of who I truly was came in fleeting moments at best. There was so much insanity in all the complaining I did in my head and to any poor soul who would lend a sympathetic ear. Gone was the loving, peaceful me.

Looking back, I see that no lower realm circumstance justifies a lower realm response. Being resentful or victimized by anyone or any situation is just a lower realm response to a lower realm situation. Period.

I've seen this sly old fox yet again. It crept up in a disguise and set up residence in my head. A stream of useless crazy thoughts overtook my being.

I intend to remain on high alert for it. Like a hunter in the woods sitting silently in a tree stand, I too will remain quiet and alert and become aware of the sly old fox as it attempts to take over my mind once again.

A man is what he thinks about all day long.
RALPH WALDO EMERSON

I INTEND TO RECOGNIZE LOWER REALM THOUGHT.

I accept the lower realm experience that resulted from my responding to a situation with judgment... *I relinquish* choosing a lower realm response in lower realm situations... *I dream of* being aware of the falseness of resentment and victimization... *With peace and love I intend to* have Awareness of Upper Realm choices... *I am grateful* to take another step up on my journey, *I am.*

The Divine Light is always in man,
presenting itself to the senses and to the comprehension,
but man rejects it.
GIORDANO BRUNO

*R*EFLECTIONS ON OPENING OURSELVES... We are infected. We are suffering the consequence of our lower realm choices. I will cease to judge. I will cease to have expectations of others. In our Oneness we will suffer and in our Oneness we will Heal. I will keep returning to Awareness. I will keep returning to Acceptance. I will keep returning to Love.

What is lovely never dies,
but passes into other loveliness,
Star-dust, or sea-foam,
flower or winged air.
THOMAS BAILEY ALDRICH

I INTEND TO BE UNCEASINGLY LOVING.

I *accept* the false beliefs and the accumulation of blockages that plague humanity... *I relinquish* fears of the darkness that shadows us... *I dream of* being a font of Love, open to all... *I dream of* being a flow of Grace... *I dream of* having a heart that is open to giving love to anyone that is yearning to remember it... *With peace and love I intend to* walk humbly and gracefully through my day with my arms and heart wide open... *I am grateful* for the healing affects of Awareness, Acceptance and Love, *I am.*

*R*EFLECTIONS ON A MAD MAD WORLD... We're all crazy. The whole lot of us! I look around at all of us and shake my head. We've been scammed. Taken in. Possessed. It's been an inside job. So we weren't even aware of the crime.

It slowly crept into our life; it became a part of us. It invaded our minds and our bodies. A true inside job. It took over our thinking. It is the lower realm thoughts of separation and judgment. It is the negative emotion that resulted from all that crazy lower realm thinking. It lives on and on in us.

Join me in becoming a private eye. A great observer. Watch yourself. Watch for it in those around you. Our greatest defense is to become Aware. Open your eyes. Distance yourself and see with new eyes. Lift the veil that obscures your vision of the Truth.

See the thoughts, see the emotions, and see what manifests as a result of it all. Just observe, don't worry about solving the crime, just study the crime scene as it unfolds before you.

I INTEND TO BE OBSERVANT.

I accept the insanity in myself and in all others... *I relinquish* fears of its affects... *I dream of* being Aware... *With peace and love I intend to* be the change I wish to see in the world... *I am grateful* to be on this path, *I am.*

He who lives in harmony with himself
lives in harmony with the world.
MARCUS AURELIUS

REFLECTIONS ON MY INNER CONFLICTS... I have been angry with so many people for their lack of respect. I've fought for respect and find myself having little solace. Fortunately, I have turned a new corner. Now instead of desiring to receive respect, I have found my own respect. I have found a deep and spiritual reverence for myself. The problem hadn't been with the rest of the world, but was a struggle within myself. It was a problem on the inside, not on the outside. I found that other people's thoughts of me were a reflection of my own thoughts. The more I thought about them not respecting me, the more they did. I was focusing my attention on what others thought instead of focusing on the only thing I really have any ability to change, my own thought.

I intend to accept that some prejudicial behaviors are just a result of our beliefs in long-held lies that have been passed down from one generation to the next. With Acceptance and Compassion there will be a transformation. I will choose to focus on the Light instead of the darkness and in doing so will strengthen Truth. My being angry with the situation was only adding darkness. I made the mistake of choosing to fight instead of choosing Awareness and Acceptance. The same conflict that I see expressed on a vast scale between nations at war.

I embrace myself. It is only in our acknowledging and embracing ourselves that we find the true strength in our Unity and Wholeness. May we cease our fight to gain respect from others and instead nourish it within ourselves.

Never violate the sacredness of your individual self-respect.
THEODORE PARKER

I INTEND TO HONOR LIFE WITH RESPECT.

I accept that some behaviors are the result of long-held beliefs passed down from one generation to the next... *I relinquish* fears of other peoples' actions affecting my inner peace... *I dream of* my light glowing strong and steady... *With peace and love I intend to* be Compassionate... *I am grateful* live in Harmony, *I am.*

When nature has work to be done,
she creates a genius to do it.
RALPH WALDO EMERSON

*R*EFLECTIONS ON CREATING OUR HOMES... I was just watching the news. Oh to witness the pain and suffering of so many souls. So much fighting over who is right and who is wrong. So many stories in our heads. So many people suffering from pain bodies that are so overwhelming.

I yearn to be strong. In the face of so much fighting, so much war, we must hold on to who we are. We must not get sucked into the insanity.

We need families. We need homes that are a beautiful expression of Life. We yearn to be nurtured by the Sacred Feminine. Let us honor the feminine by being beautiful.

Open your arms, your hearts and the doors to your homes. Receive all who come. Welcome them all. Nurture them so that we can be whole.

The deepest experience of the creator is feminine,
for it is experience of receiving and bearing.
RAINER MARIA RILKE

I INTEND TO EMBRACE THE SACRED FEMININE.

I accept my femininity... *I relinquish* fears that to be feminine is to be weak... *I dream of* becoming aware of the beauty, strength and power that are inherent in the Feminine... *With peace and love I intend to* honor Life... *I am grateful* to create a home that nurtures Connection, *I am.*

*R*EFLECTIONS ON MY BRAIN… This morning in meditation there was stillness, there was space, vastness. For the last two months that space was filled with an endless stream of thought. One thought after another. My mind was restless. It would find another idea, like a toy, and want to play with it, analyze it, brood over it, expand on it…

It is exhausting. I won't judge what has happened. I will just become Aware. Observe it. Let it be. Awareness and Acceptance will settle it down.

I INTEND TO RETURN TO STILLNESS.

I accept the flaring of lower realm thoughts and emotions… *I relinquish* fears of being a failure… *I dream of* once again sensing the Divine… *With peace and love I intend to* be patient… *I am grateful* to return to Stillness, *I am.*

A sick thought can devour the body's flesh more than fever or consumption.
GUY DE MAUPASSANT

REFLECTIONS ON MY RISING... When I wake in the morning often times the monkey mind is what wakes me. I think my body would welcome a little more sleep, but my brain switches on and instead I lay there thinking uselessly of this and that. Pointless mental chatter. If my mind gets carried away, I will abruptly get out of bed to start the day. I essentially attempt to interrupt the 'monkey mind.'

The brain can be so useful until it gets taken over by obsessive thought. Obsessively thinking is an addiction. It's too much of something that could be good in moderation. Too much food, too much alcohol, too much thought. Addiction is painful. I'm ready to get this monkey off of my back.

I've had glimpses of a wonderfully expansive mind. It is a Peaceful Presence. I wish to live in that state. I wish for us all to live in that state of Being. Every time I notice a stream of lower realm thought I'm going to center myself and watch it. Then once again I will humbly ask for healing. "Please heal my mind."

It is in your power to withdraw yourself
whenever you desire.
Perfect tranquility within
consists in the good ordering of the mind,
the realm of your own.
MARCUS AURELIUS

I INTEND TO RECEIVE HEALING.

I accept the pointless mental chatter... *I relinquish* fears of it never going away... *I dream of* remembering that healing is always available to me... *With peace and love I intend to* enjoy the bliss of a tranquil presence... *I am grateful* for Stillness within, *I am.*

No act of kindness,
no matter how small,
is ever wasted.
AESOP

REFLECTIONS ON ENTERTAINING... I've added another aspect to my preparations for welcoming people into my home. In the past I would cook, clean and arrange the house and its pretties all in an effort to create a welcoming atmosphere.

Now I want to add to my entertaining to do list: "-create an atmosphere of Peace and Acceptance conducive to spreading Joy."

I want to provide more than just snack mix for hungry tummies; I want to provide love for hungry souls. I want to provide more than just refreshments for parched mouths; I want to provide compassion for weary souls plagued by falseness and pain.

The manner of giving
is worth more than the gift.
PIERRE CORNEILLE

I INTEND TO HONOR THE GIFT OF NURTURING.

I accept the tasks of life bringer, nourisher, leader... *I relinquish* beliefs in thoughts of inadequacy... *I dream of* remembering that my cup is filled from the inexhaustible Source... *With peace and I intend to* honor all who are called to be Kind... *I am grateful* to be Graceful, *I am.*

What would life be
if we had no courage to attempt anything?
VINCENT VAN GOGH

REFLECTIONS ON PIONEERING... We are pioneers venturing into a new territory. Sometimes we may want to turn back, head east back to the comforts of civilization to what is familiar and easy. But no, we must choose to do what we know needs to be done. We must choose to venture into a new land. We must choose a new way of life. We will have the courage to choose to Live Beautifully and we will reach out our hand to all who choose to join us.

The giant oak is an acorn
that held its ground.
ENGLISH PROVERB

I INTEND TO BE COURAGEOUS.

I accept that tomorrow can be as I dream it to be... *I relinquish* fears of needing to hold on to old patterns... *I dream of* having the courage to blaze a new trail... *With peace and love I intend to* hold out a hand to all who wish to join me... *I am grateful* for new beginnings, *I am.*

What we see
depends mainly on what we look for.
JOHN LUBBOCK

*R*EFLECTIONS ON BLOCKAGES... When I first became aware of fear I saw it in all its really grandiose circumstances like war and crime. As I continue to be attentive I see it in varying degrees all over the place. Fears in the form of worry, doubt, guilt, embarrassment, anxiety, unworthiness, judgment, expectation... I see the results of our fearful thinking; so many blockages to the Love that yearns to flow.

Turn your face to the sun
and the shadows fall behind you.
MAORI PROVERB

I INTEND TO HAVE THE COURAGE TO ASK FOR LOVE.

I accept life as it is... *I relinquish* fears of being unworthy of Grace... *I dream of* all of mankind choosing Love... *With peace and love I intend to* be an expression of Love so that all that I think, and speak and do will be a blessing... *I am grateful* for the gift of Life, *I am.*

REFLECTIONS ON OUR RELATIONSHIPS... I see that I am plagued by the false-ness of expecting my 'elders' or 'superiors' to be the ones to lead the way on this journey. I see that I am plagued by the falseness of thinking that I am justified in being resentful towards them for not paving the way for me. I see them through the lens of this falseness. I look through these clouded glasses and feel justified putting up boundaries of protection against the lower realm choices that they make over and over again. I wonder if they are looking at me and thinking the same thing. I see how this attitude keeps us stuck in the muck. Stuck in the muck of being sick and tired of having to put up with everyone else's crap. I am ready to get out of the muck.

I INTEND TO ACCEPT OTHERS EXACTLY AS THEY ARE.

I *accept* my relationships with others... *I relinquish* fears of being affected by their crap... *I dream of* seeing through the layers of fear to their souls... *I dream of* truly accepting them as they are... *With peace and love I intend to* walk through my day seeking only to Love... *I am grateful* to be Compassionate, *I am.*

Be patient and tough;
one day this pain will be useful to you.
OVID

REFLECTIONS ON MY WOUNDS... I see that I have put up walls of protection. My wounds are the places where I didn't know how to love. I see that the walls must come down. Slowly and steadily I will become aware of all of the 'places' where I feel justified in putting up a wall of protection. I will grow. I honor myself with the time and effort it takes to grow. I will heal and I then I will remember.

May today there be peace within.
May you trust God that you are exactly where you are meant to be.
May you not forget the infinite possibilities that are born of faith.
May you use those gifts that you have received,
and pass on the love that has been given to you.
May you be content knowing you are a child of God.
Let this presence settle into your bones,
and allow your soul the freedom to sing, dance, praise and love.
ST. TERESA OF AVILA

I INTEND TO KNOW THAT I AM WORTHY OF LOVE.

I *accept* that I have felt unworthy... *I relinquish* belief in thoughts that anything could make me unworthy of being loved and supported... *I dream of* being healed of the error in my thinking... *I dream of* my mind being healed and the truth of my worthiness being restored to my knowing... *With peace and love I intend to* be compassionate towards myself and all others who have forgotten how perfect they are... *I am grateful* for becoming aware of my life experiences that made wounds, *I am.*

I have been driven many times upon my knees
by the overwhelming conviction that I had no where else to go.
My own wisdom and that of all about me
seemed insufficient for that day.
ABRAHAM LINCOLN

*R*EFLECTIONS ON SURRENDER… I'm falling apart physically. So I must be mentally and emotionally. What's up? Instead of creating with power, I'm wanting. I'm wanting to help this person. I'm wanting to change things. I'm wanting to get this and that done. Wanting comes from fearful thoughts.

No more wanting. Instead I choose to create what I yearn for with Love. Love won't come through me unless I let go of controlling out of fear. Grace won't come through me until I let go of wanting out of fear. It's not about working hard or in the right way. It's just about walking gently through life aligning myself with the Divine, choosing to create with Love.

It is foolish to think that we will enter heaven
without entering into ourselves.
ST. TERESA OF AVILA

I INTEND TO RETURN TO THE GARDEN.

I accept the error of my ways… *I relinquish* wanting… *I dream of* creating with Love… *With peace and love I intend to* let go of the illusion of controlling out of fear and instead cherish the joy of creating with Love… *I am grateful* to experience Heaven on Earth as the falseness falls away, *I am.*

The key to change…
is to let go of fear.
ROSANNE CASH

*R*EFLECTIONS ON POISON… Everything that isn't loving in my life feels poisonous. Any moment spent being anything but loving feels vulgar. It's just wrong. It harms me. So it is with any moment not being joyful. I feel repulsed by it.

There are relationships with unhealthy patterns of thoughts and behaviors that I have been in for so long. There is a part of me that is so stubborn, I want to keep struggling to get it right.

But there is a new part of me that knows I'll never experience Peace through stubbornness and struggle. I'll only get there through Acceptance and Love.

Now that I am aware of the struggles, I wish to let them go. If I experience a struggle, I know it is a step in the wrong direction.

Please grant me the wisdom to walk away from pain. I wish to leave the struggles behind and create a life of Love and Joy!

Receive with simplicity
everything that happens to you.
RASHI

I INTEND TO BE OPEN TO WHAT IS.

I accept that I believed that 'success' came from hard work and determination… *I relinquish* fears that life will never change… *I dream of* being Aware of how tense I am feeling when I believe fearful lower realm thoughts… *With peace and love I intend to* create a beautiful life by choosing Acceptance… *I am grateful* to realize that growth occurs in openness, *I am.*

It is the nature of things to be drawn to the very experiences
that will spoil our innocence,
transform our lives,
and give us necessary complexity and depth.
THOMAS MOORE

REFLECTIONS ON A CHANGING TIDE... I'm letting go. I'm willing to let go of areas of my life that aren't joyful. I'm willing to accept the uncertainty that comes with change. In taking the steps in my life of letting go, I feel a release in my body. What's happening? Have I had emotional blockages that manifest as physical blockages? Are they too releasing? Does the physical always follow the emotional? Does the emotion always follow the thought?

I'm seeing the world as just forms of energy. How do I see it so differently than the people around me and not feel alienated? Do I remain quiet in my knowing, relaxed in the gently unfolding of humanity? Things take time. It's okay. Focus on yourself Doris. The love that results will affect others.

Nothing in life is to be feared,
it is only to be understood.
Now is the time to understand more,
so that we may fear less.
MARIE CURIE

I INTEND TO BE A LOVING PRESENCE.

I accept the gentle unfolding of us all... *I relinquish* belief in thoughts that I am not doing enough, soon enough, fast enough, for enough... *I dream of* humanity Living Beautifully... *With peace and love I intend to* create a beautiful life that ripples out and affects humanity... *I am grateful* to be aware that I am a point of Union between my Heavenly Father and my Earthly Mother, *I am.*

It is love alone
that gives worth to all things.
ST. TERESA OF AVILA

$\mathcal{R}$EFLECTIONS ON SHARING... As a woman, a mother, and a wife, I am programmed to be a caregiver. Whenever I see a need I feel a pull to reach out and help. As I've learned about the affects of fear and love, of pain bodies, of awareness, of our monkey minds, I see the love in others and I also see the pain. I want to reach out and make a difference.

I yearn to have a healing presence; pure sweet, beautiful energy flowing endlessly from my heart. I yearn to be a source of Love in whatever the moment asks. My 'to do' list includes letting go of every cloud that obscures the Light that shines from within me. I will keep asking for Grace. I will keep receiving the gift.

I pray that the Grace will radiate like the rays of the sun.

It is difficult to make a man miserable
while he feels worthy of himself
and claims kindred to the great God who made him.
ABRAHAM LINCOLN

I INTEND TO RESONATE LOVE.

I accept our journeys exactly as they are... *I relinquish* fears of my loved ones' journeys... *I dream of* being a source of beautiful Love... *With peace and love I intend to* share Joy... *I am grateful* for being aware of the most powerful force, *I am... I am grateful* to be aware of Love, *I am.*

Men, it has been well said, think in herds, and it will be seen that they will go mad in herds, while they only recover their senses slowly, and one by one.
CHARLES MACKAY

*R*EFLECTIONS ON UNITY... I just ran an errand. It's an autumn day. On the way home I drove down a country road with yellowed corn creating walls alongside me and an open blue sky above. I came upon a flock of blackbirds flying over the cornfield as graceful and moving as the dance of the sugar plum fairies.

I've been so enamored by blackbirds lately. They fly in flocks at this time of year. They can all be perched in trees in my backyard, literally hundreds of them and all at one time they seem to decide to get up and fly to another destination. You would think that they would be flying into each other, colliding. You would think that there would be confusion as to which way they are going to go.

But there isn't. They seem to operate as individual birds and yet also as one flock. The flock seems to have one mind and they all seem to have access to this one mind.

If we could stand back from mankind, would we look like a flock? Individuals part of a collective Whole? All moving in unison towards a common destination?

We feel so alone, so isolated in our illusion of separateness. Have we lost the knowing of our Oneness? Are we individual birds within a beautiful flock ignorant of our Unity? Thoughts and feelings of separateness and isolation being not our reality, but a result of our ignorance?

Make my joy complete by being of the same mind, maintaining the same love, united in spirit, intent on one purpose.
PHILIPPIANS 4:2

I INTEND TO SENSE THE TRUTH OF THE ONENESS OF ALL.

I accept that we have largely lost the knowledge of our Oneness... *I relinquish* beliefs in thoughts of being alone... *I relinquish* beliefs in thoughts of being separate... *I relinquish* beliefs in thoughts of being incomplete... *I relinquish* beliefs in thoughts of needing someone... *I dream of* the Truth of our Oneness being revealed in our hearts... *With peace and love I intend to* extend Compassion to every member of our flock, so that we might recall the Love that we have strayed from and once again remember our Oneness... *I am grateful* for the pain of separation to be slowly receding, *I am.*

It is our attitude towards events, not events themselves, which we can control.
Nothing is by its own nature calamitous—
even death is terrible only if we fear it.
EPICTETUS

REFLECTIONS ON GETTING THE JOB DONE... So often I set off to accomplish something with my own determination and strength. I work hard at bringing about change for the greater good. Do I get a good result? I'm not so sure. The results could be much better if I would learn to open myself to allow for a stream of endless Love to come through me. I call it 'being in the Flow.'

My true strength comes not from my own doing, but from my surrendering control and instead opening myself and asking for the Flow to come through me. When I'm in the Flow, Love, Joy and Compassion emanate from my being. There is no effort, just a surrender, a softening, a release of the blockages that otherwise would obscure it; an openness that allows the Flow to come through.

What does it take to live in this state of openness? Surrender. Surrender the illusion of controlling your life. Then humbly ask for and receive the Flow. Every day ask. Every day receive.

Welcome all who come to you with open arms so that they might receive the warmth of the Love that flows through you.

This grace of God is a very great, strong, mighty and active thing.
It does not lie asleep in the soul.
Grace hears, leads, drives, draws, changes, works all in man,
and lets itself be distinctly felt and experienced.
It is hidden, but its works are evident.
MARTIN LUTHER

I INTEND TO LIVE IN THE FLOW.

I accept that I have lived with dis-ease... *I relinquish* the false beliefs of lacking what I need... *I dream of* knowing that I can relax in the Flow of support from our Earthly Mother... *With peace and love I intend* to give thanks each and every day for being loved and supported... *I am grateful* to live at ease in the Flow of Life that supports my every need, *I am.*

Compassion is the basis for morality.
ARTHUR SCHOPENHAUER

*R*EFLECTIONS ON COMPASSION FOR ALL... I see that I am not alone on the Journey. Please bless us all with healed minds. Please bless us all with hearts overflowing with Compassion and Love. Please bless all of our creations this day. Please bless us all that we might be one beautiful Light in this world.

If your compassion does not include yourself,
it is incomplete.
BUDDHA

I INTEND TO BE COMPASSIONATE.

I *accept* that all of humanity is on a spiritual journey... *I accept* that we are in this together... *I relinquish* fears of others peoples' choices in life causing me pain... *I dream of* healing for us all... *With peace and love I intend to* know that my discomfort is an indication that I have strayed from the Truth of creating with Love... *I am grateful* for moments when I remember to ask for Grace for all of humanity, *I am.*

There are some wounds that one can heal only by deepening them
and making them worse.
VILLIERS DE L'ISLE-ADAM

EFLECTIONS ON LOVE... I see that I came into this life with lessons to learn. I see that we are learning together. We are learning how to be endless expressions of Love. If there is tension, it's just a wound within us where the Love doesn't flow. Yet another of life's lessons to learn, another wound, another elephant in the room that must be faced with courage.

If you want to shrink something,
You must first allow it to expand.
If you want to get rid of something,
You must first allow it to flourish.
If you want to take something,
You must first allow it to be given.
This is called the subtle perception,
Of the way things are.
LAOZI
TAO TE CHING, TRANSLATED BY STEPHEN MITCHELL

I INTEND TO BE AWARE OF FEELING JUSTIFIED
IN PROTECTING MY WOUNDS.

I accept that I have put up walls where I am unaware of how to respond with Love... I *relinquish* fears of any relationship that comes my way... I *dream of* our wounds being healed... *With peace and love I intend to* perceive the innocence of all who cross my path... *I am grateful* to be vulnerable, to set down my armor and to look with Awareness, *I am.*

REFLECTIONS ON BEING IN HARMONY… I see that my life is a pursuit of living in harmony. Choices that feel bad are a step away from harmony. Choices that feel good are a step towards greater harmony. I see that my yearning to live in the Upper Realm is a yearning to resonate with Love. I see that the journey is one of letting go of all that blocks my capacity to sing a sweet song in Union with All.

Heaven, to me,
is the complete synchronization with higher frequencies
and vibrations of creation being totally entrained.
In other words,
being at-one-ment.
DAVID HULSE, D.D.

I INTEND TO BE AWARE OF WHAT I FEEL.

I accept that we, every single human being on this planet, are a part of a collective Whole… *I accept* that I have felt separate and afraid… *I accept* that every single one of us was made from one cloth and we are all struggling to return to knowing our Oneness… *I relinquish* judgmental thoughts that result in lower realm emotions that are an indication that I am living in darkness… *I dream of* living in the Light… *I dream of* knowing of the Oneness of All… *With peace and love I intend to* devote myself to being aware of my emotions… *I am grateful* to live in a state of Love, *I am.*

REFLECTIONS ON THE DANCE... We're all dancing to the beat of a beautiful song called Life. The song has many refrains. At times we dance to the beat of pure joy, at other times in our life the melody is one of sorrow.

Whatever the tempo may be, accept it and participate fully in the dance. Dance alone, dance with a partner, or dance with the whole world... Feel the beat of the music in every cell of your body. Embrace the music. If you choose to only experience certain emotions, your song will be dull and monotone. No, live fully in the moment, whatever that may be. Embrace life, be it joy, love or sorrow.

Dance with me my friends. Dance!

I INTEND TO JOIN FULLY IN THE DANCE.

I accept every one of my experiences knowing that they all hold precious life lessons... *I relinquish* believing that any moment isn't right... *I dream of* opening myself to dance with unbridled fervor to whatever music is playing in my life at any given moment... *With peace and love I intend to* accept others around me that are dancing to their own beat... *I am grateful* for life exactly as it is, *I am.*

When an idea
exclusively occupies the mind,
it is transformed
into an actual physical or mental state.
SWAMI VIVEKANANDA

REFLECTIONS ON MY STATE OF BEING... I see how beliefs affect my body. I see that when I believe the thoughts of blame, scarcity and unworthiness it results in feeling physically bad. I see that when I choose thoughts of Self-Respect, Self-Worth and Self-Love it results in feeling good. I see that my thoughts lead to emotions and my physical body is a reflection of those emotions. I see the thinking that results in health and vitality. I see the thinking that results in physical decline.

Kindness is a language
which the deaf can hear
and the blind can see.
MARK TWAIN

I INTEND TO BE A REFLECTION OF KINDNESS.

I *accept* that my body reflects what is going on in my head... *I relinquish* believing every thought that crosses my mind... *I dream of* being aware of my power to choose what I believe... *With peace and love I intend to* be Kind and Compassionate... *I am grateful* to realize that when I choose the Upper Realm, my body opens up (creation) and when I choose the lower realm, my body closes down (separation), *I am.*

He who kneels the most,
stands the best.
D. L. MOODY

*R*EFLECTIONS ON MY DAILY RITUAL... Last night I returned home from visiting college campuses with my youngest daughter. On top of my travel fatigue, my husband woke at 3:45 a.m. with a horrible Charlie horse. I woke to rub his leg and try to help him work out the cramp. Afterwards, it took me quite awhile to get back to sleep. Finally I did and I slept right through my time for prayer and meditation. We intended to leave in an hour for our son's college football game, but here I sit in my chair. Oh, the dilemma.

I have come to realize that a day without the Grace that comes from the time spent in prayer and meditation is not the life I choose. Without it my day is flat. I would rather wake early and get less sleep in order to be able to take the opportunity for prayer and meditation. I would rather be late for the game, than skip this time for Connection. It is the perfect, no, it is the only way to start a day.

If I don't wake early enough, there are people and activities that may interrupt my Bliss. I will choose. I will choose to rise early. My morning ritual is the most precious and necessary gift, the opportunity to empty my mind and sit in Stillness. It opens my mind, it cleanses my being, and it creates a great vastness of space within me. I sit in prayer. I ask for Grace. I ask to be of service. I ask for Healing. And then, in the true spirit of giving, I do my best to become a gracious receiver. The asking comes easy, the giving comes instantly, my openness to receiving needs work.

Do not have your concert first,
and then tune your instrument afterwards.
Begin the day with the Word of God and prayer,
and get first of all into harmony with Him.
JAMES HUDSON TAYLOR

I INTEND TO BE COMMITTED TO CONNECTING.
I accept that there are blockages within me that need to be healed... *I relinquish* fears of the Journey... *I dream of* clarity... *With peace and love I intend to* begin my day with Connection and Awareness... *I am grateful* to be committed, *I am.*

How far that little candle throws his beams!
So shines a good deed in a weary world.
WILLIAM SHAKESPEARE

REFLECTIONS ON OUR RAYS OF LIGHT... Each of us is a beacon. A source of Light. Fears are like an accumulation of grime on the glass. The Light still exists, but its rays can't escape to reach out into the world. As we heal our minds we stop adding to the grime, and as we forgive ourselves the glass clears and the Light is able to escape out into the world. We become beacons of Light, lighthouses for others to see. Just as lighthouse keepers work diligently to let their lights shine, let us do the same.

PHOSPHORESCENCE.
Now there's a word to lift your hat to...
to find that phosphorescence,
that light within,
that's the genius behind poetry.
EMILY DICKINSON

I INTEND TO BE A BEACON OF LIGHT.
I accept the task of cleaning up my mind and cleaning up my body... *I relinquish* holding on to fears and the consequences of the errors of the past... *I dream of* being aware, asking for the healing of my mind and asking for the undoing of the circumstances of my past errors... *With peace and love I intend to* ask for healing and forgiveness... *I am grateful* for the gift of clarity and order, *I am.*

When you reach the heart of life
you shall find beauty in all things,
even in the eyes that are blind to beauty.
KAHLIL GIBRAN

REFLECTIONS ON REMEMBERING WHO I AM... It is so very humbling to know in your heart just how beautiful you are. As I see my judgmental thoughts, and as I realize that they are errors, they begin to fall away. It leaves me with only what is real; with the knowing that I am a beautiful creation. Absolutely beautiful. As the falsehoods gently fall away, my loving Being is free to shine.

To be in the presence of Love is so very humbling. It was there all the time. I had just developed so many fearful thought patterns that clouded and kept me in the dark, that I couldn't sense the real me.

I pray for healing, for myself and all others. I pray that our minds be healed so that we can remember once again who we truly are. I pray for healing so that we can remember how beautiful we are. I pray for healing so that we can love purely and beautifully. I pray that we might live our lives honoring the Guidance that is given and being open to receiving the creation of the Inspirations.

One by one let us shed our lower realm beliefs. Let us see them and let them gently fall away. Let us be radiant beacons of Love and Light, just as we were created.

Everything has beauty,
but not everyone sees it.
CONFUCIUS

I INTEND TO SENSE MY RADIANCE.

I accept the illusion that blinds myself and others... *I relinquish* judging our blindness... *I dream of* us all having eyes that see... *With peace and love I intend to* see only the Radiance in us all... *I am grateful* to see Truth, *I am.*

No one is useless in the world
who lightens the burdens of another.
CHARLES DICKENS

*R*EFLECTIONS ON BEING GRACEFUL... I want to learn to be a receiver. I want to make the choice everyday to ask for Grace.

Please join me my friends in creating the world we yearn to live in; a world of Peace and Love. Ask each and every day to be open to Grace. Ask for Peace and Love to come through you. Each and every day honor the Guidance for being the perfect expression of your authenticity.

Christ went more willingly to the cross than we do to the throne of grace.
THOMAS WATSON

I INTEND TO ASK FOR GRACE.

I accept that I must ask each day... *I relinquish* beliefs of being unworthy... *With peace and love I intend to* ask for Grace each and every day... *I am grateful* to know that I am a child of the Divine, *I am.*

One day at a time—this is enough.
Do not look back and grieve over the past
for it is gone;
and do not be troubled about the future,
for it has not yet come.
Live in the present,
and make it so beautiful
it will be worth remembering.
IDA SCOTT TAYLOR

*R*EFLECTIONS ON OUR RISING... I accept that we have been attempting to gain control of our lives as a result of the fears that stem from feeling separate from God, from feeling separate from the Whole.

But there is a stirring. We can feel it. We are on the brink of a rebirth. It's like we retreated to the dark of the deep woods to hide from persecution. We've lain silent and still in the leaves beneath the large oak tree waiting for the moment when we could rise up and walk the earth once more and create our lives with Truth. We are stirring. There is movement on the forest floor. A new creation is ready to emerge.

People who understand the beauty of their feminineness... Beautiful people who accept the wonderful energies of our earth and nourish those who yearn for it... Beautiful people who choose to be loving and graceful each and every day...

Stretch your legs my friends. We have something to rise up and do. We are ready to heal the minds and hearts of mankind with the Light of Awareness.

Though my soul may set in darkness,
it will rise in perfect light.
I have loved the stars too fondly
to be fearful of the night.
SARAH WILLIAMS

I INTEND TO RISE IN GLORY.

I accept our journey... *I relinquish* fears of being persecuted for being who I am... *I dream of* being graceful and loving... *I dream of* expressing Truth... *With peace and love I intend to* be rooted to the Feminine... *I am grateful* for Life, *I am*.

Because one believes in oneself,
one doesn't try to convince others.
Because one is content with oneself,
one doesn't need others' approval.
Because one accepts oneself,
the whole world accepts him or her.
LAOZI

*R*EFLECTIONS ON A NEW ME... I feel like I am changing. I look different. I feel different. Old ways feel like they don't fit. Old clothes don't fit.

I love the new me. I am calm and centered. I am graceful and poised. I am a shining light... a source of Acceptance and Love. I know what I want and have the courage to not look to others for validation. I am comfortable in my own skin.

Welcome home sunshine.

First say to yourself
what you would be;
and then do
what you have to do.
EPICTETUS

I INTEND TO BE COMFORTABLE IN MY OWN SKIN.

I accept that I have conformed to societies' norms to avoid judgment... *I relinquish* honoring thoughts of doubt... *I dream of* being comfortable expressing myself authentically... *With peace and love I intend to* express myself with honesty... *I am grateful* to know that I am perfectly me, *I am.*

Acceptance of others,
their looks,
their behaviors,
their beliefs,
bring you an inner peace and tranquility—
instead of anger and resentment.
UNKNOWN

REFLECTIONS ON HEALING... We can remain blocked remembering our many wounds or we can rise up and let the wounds fall away. We can rise up in our glory with outstretched arms open to be healed by Compassion and Love.

In our quiet moments of solitude we can pray. We can pray that we will all be blessed with Grace, that we will all be Healed. We can pray that we will listen and respond to Guidance to nurture, heal and love each other.

Never be in a hurry;
do everything quietly
and in a calm spirit.
Do not lose your inner peace for anything whatsoever,
even if your whole world seems upset.
ST. FRANCIS DE SALES

I INTEND TO HEAL WITH COMPASSION.

I accept this moment in the unending unfolding... *I accept* that the parts that are uncomfortable are just places that are in need of healing Grace; just places that are a call for prayer... *I relinquish* fears of my perceptions of the shortcomings of others... *I dream of* healing for us all... *With peace and love I intend* to open my heart and my arms... *With peace and love I intend to* be an opening of Love, Grace and Healing... *I am grateful* for Compassion, *I am.*

I sought to hear the voice of God
and climbed the topmost steeple,
but God declared:
"Go down again—
I dwell among the people."
JOHN HENRY NEWMAN

*R*EFLECTIONS ON OUR TEMPLES… Often times I yearn to kiss a child on the temples. What is this yearning? Why am I so drawn to their temples and to the crowns of their heads? Temples and crowns. Are these places of glory? Are these openings where Grace enters us readily?

I will act on my yearnings. Maybe they are a response to a need for the healing that comes from motherly love. I will honor my yearnings as pulls and tugs on my heartstrings when a soul is in need of an outpouring of healing love.

I will be comfortable expressing myself. The world is yearning for love. I will respond to my maternal instincts to heal with a hug and a kiss.

True glory consists in doing what deserves to be written,
in writing what deserves to be read,
and in so living
as to make the world happier and better for our living in it.
PLINY THE ELDER

I INTEND TO HEAL WITH ACTS OF LOVE.

I accept that humanity is sometimes reluctant to express love… *I relinquish* fears of expressing myself… *I dream of* my love healing others… *With peace and love I intend to* respond to Guidance… *I am grateful* for love that is shared, *I am.*

Come forth into the light of things,
let nature be your teacher.
WILLIAM WORDSWORTH

ℛEFLECTIONS ON AN OPENING... I feel myself changing. There is a shift, a movement within me. I'm beginning to accept my husband exactly as he is, not wishing for anything different. I'm ready to open myself to receive him. To truly connect in a union of two souls. I'm ready to let fall away the parts that block it. The parts that have kept me from completely receiving him just as he is.

I feel like I'm opening to receive him in a new way physically as well. There has been a tightness and sometimes pain in my pelvic region for so long. A restriction.

Is that inherited tightness that resulted from generations of women who slowly protected themselves from unloving unions of men and women? Did the beautiful union of man and woman turn into the ugly taking of women? Do we build walls of protection where others have attempted to take from us?

I want to let the past fall away. I want to start anew. I want to be open to joining in a union that is free from walls that block the flow of Love.

Love conquers all things;
let us too surrender to Love.
VIRGIL

I INTEND TO SURRENDER HABITS OF CONTROLLING OUT OF FEAR.

I accept what has transpired between generations of men and women... *I relinquish* fears of the past continuing to repeat itself... *I dream of* human sexuality being a beautiful reflection of Truth and Love... *With peace and love I intend to* open up to giving and receiving Love... *I am grateful* for the walls that are crumbling, *I am.*

No man is a true believer
unless he desireth for his brother
that which he desireth for himself.
MUHAMMAD

REFLECTIONS ON OUR FAMILIES... I accept that humanity is afflicted by false fearful beliefs. And so we suffer. Each one of us is yearning to love and to be loved, but our minds are plagued by false lower realm thinking that clouds our knowing of who and what we truly are.

What can we do? We can choose to ask for healing for ourselves and our loved ones. Instead of trying to work things out or think things through, we can to turn to prayer. We can ask for Healing for all. We have the option of honoring the inspirations to Live Beautifully or to take control with an iron-clad determination.

It is surely better to pardon too much,
than to condemn too much.
GEORGE ELLIOT

I INTEND TO ASK FOR GRACE FOR ALL.

I accept that humanity is afflicted with false beliefs and the consequences of believing them... *I relinquish* responding to the lower realm circumstances with anger and resentment... *I dream of* being Compassionate.... *With peace and love I intend to* ask for Healing for myself and for all others by responding to suffering as if it is a plea for someone to call 911, a plea for someone to humbly fall to ones' knees to request the gift of Grace from God and all of the angels, the gift of Light, the gift of Healing... *I am grateful* for Forgiveness, *I am.*

I swear to you that to think too much is a disease,
a real, actual disease.
FYODOR DOSTOYEVSKY

*R*EFLECTIONS ON A DAY GONE BAD... Wow what a day yesterday was. Craziness. I went from sheer joy at lunch time to a crazy emotional episode by evening.

What happened to knock me so far off center? What choice caused me to move from Peace and Joy to frantic thoughts and emotions?

When I was faced with someone's pain and emotion I caught it like a bad cold. I reacted to the situation with negative thoughts and judgments. I wish I would have noticed the negative thinking and taken a moment to ask for Healing. But I didn't and once it got started it grew to epic proportions.

Never open the door to a lesser evil,
for other and greater ones invariably slink in after it.
BALTASAR GRACIAN

I INTEND TO BE AWARE OF DARKNESS.

I accept that we suffer when we are plagued with 'ick'... *I accept* that the darkness will cease to be as we come to recognize it... *I relinquish* fears of its affect on me... *I dream of* humanity choosing to ask for Healing and for Guidance and choosing to create our lives with Love... *I dream of* our knowing of our Oneness... *I dream of* humanity being blessed with Healing... *I dream of* humanity being blessed with Joy... *I dream of* humanity being blessed with Grace and with Beauty... *With peace and love I intend to* remain attentive to perpetually asking for Guidance, expressing the Guidance with language, and then acting with Faith... *I am grateful* for the knowing that we are blessed with the choice to receive Healing, Joy, Grace and Beauty, *I am.*

If the only prayer you said in your whole life was,
"thank you,"
that would suffice.
MEISTER ECKHART

ℛEFLECTIONS ON A DAY OF GRATITUDE... I give thanks. No, more than that. Thanks seems to come from my head. This runs deeper. Gratitude. Gratitude seems to come from my heart.

I sit in a space of humbleness and gratitude for the blessings in my life. For the beautiful home we live in. It is our nest. A warm, cozy place that is lined with softness. For the loved ones who flock to our nest to gather together. For the beautiful feasts that I lay on our table. For the food that nourishes our bodies with health and vitality allowing us to live and love in this world. For this and so much more, I give thanks. I sit in the expansiveness of my gratitude and marvel at the beauty of life.

True happiness is to enjoy the present,
without anxious dependence upon the future,
not to amuse ourselves with either hopes or fears
but to rest satisfied with what we have,
which is sufficient,
for he that is so wants nothing.
The greatest blessings of mankind are within us and within our reach.
A wise man is content with his lot,
whatever it may be,
without wishing for what he has not.
LUCIUS ANNAEUS SENECA

I INTEND TO CREATE WITH A GRATEFUL HEART.

I accept the blessing of my home... *I relinquish* fears of being 'unworthy' of my stuff... *I dream of* my physical expression being an outward expression of a beautiful inner me... *With peace and love I intend to* honor beautiful expressions... *I am grateful* to open my eyes and sense the Truth of enjoying Creation, *I am.*

Your task is not to seek for love,
but merely to seek and find all the barriers within yourself
that you have built against it.
JALAL AD-DIN RUMI

REFLECTIONS ON BEING VULNERABLE... I see that there is a blockage in me that generates fears of opening up. I see that there once were lower realm experiences that I didn't know how to react to with Love. So I set up boundaries. Walls. It is like I was a child not yet capable of handling a situation and so I had to limit where I could go. Since then, Life has given me experiences from which I have grown. I find myself back in the place where I once built a wall.

All walls must come down. The Garden has no walls of protection. I must take down the boundaries, the walls, and face the lower realm situations with an Upper Realm response. I must be vulnerable. I must go to the places where I have been burned in the past. I must go to a place that I have deemed a Danger Zone. I will go back into the fire with Faith in knowing that I am protected by a new shield, Love.

Courage is resistance to fear,
mastery of fear,
not absence of fear.
MARK TWAIN

I INTEND TO KNOW THAT LOVE KNOWS NO BOUNDARIES.

I *accept* that I have built walls... *I relinquish* holding on to walls that are no longer needed for protection... *I dream of* having the courage to be vulnerable... *With peace and love I intend to* know that I have the strength to quietly remain in the Upper Realm despite the lower realm circumstances that swirl around me... *I am grateful* that the walls around my heart are tumbling down, *I am.*

My destination is no longer a place,
rather a new way of seeing.
MARCEL PROUST

*R*EFLECTIONS ON MY LIFE AS IT IS... I choose to no longer label situations as good or bad. Things just are. Life gives me the perfect circumstances for the evolution of my soul. Struggle is just a time for new growth.

I will accept the changes that will be necessary for this growth. I will be Aware of the times when I perceive circumstances to be adverse. I will respond with awareness in the face of my perception of adversity. The circumstances will cease to be adverse when I stop judging.

If you try to cure evil with evil
you will add more pain to your fate.
SOPHOCLES

I INTEND TO CHOOSE UPPER REALM RESPONSES
TO LOWER REALM SITUATIONS.

I *accept* my life as it is... *I accept* my life as it has been... *I relinquish* responding with fear to any circumstances in life... *I dream of* living without judgment of what is... *I dream of* seeing fear, denying the temptation to responding to it with more of the same, and instead choosing Awareness... *With peace and love I intend to* walk through my day with Acceptance of all that is... *I am grateful* to see the falseness of feeling justified in judging, *I am.*

REFLECTIONS ON BEING IMPECCABLE WITH YOUR WORD... I see that what we say can be a blessing or a curse. I will seek kindness in every moment. I will think kind thoughts. I will feel kind. I will be kind. I will speak kind words. In doing so, I will honor my choice to Live Beautifully.

I INTEND TO SPEAK WITH KINDNESS.

I *accept* that anything akin to Beauty, Kindness, Love, Compassion and Joy are all I wish to ever create in my thoughts and in my expressions... *I relinquish* thoughts, speech and actions that are fearful... *I dream of* creating Beauty every moment of my life... *With peace and love I intend to* be Kind... *I am grateful* to know that I have a choice to honor Inspiration with Love or to attempt to control out of fear, *I am.*

The winds of grace are blowing all the time.
You have only to raise your sail.
RAMAKRISHNA

REFLECTIONS ON A WATERFALL... God yearns to give abundantly. God is just waiting for us to clear the space and ask. So clear a space, relinquish something that no longer serves you and then ask for something else to take its place. Relinquish fear and ask for Love. Relinquish pain and ask for Faith. Relinquish judgment and ask for Peace.

Like a passionate gorgeous woman in the old movies, reach out and clear off the table before you with one big dramatic sweep of your outstretched arm. Let the crap fall away wherever it may. Clear the space. Open yourself for new possibilities of Abundance and Joy.

After your Hollywood-style outburst, return to the quiet you and fall to your knees and ask. Ask for something new; a new way of life. Ask for Peace, Love and Joy. Keep asking for more and more. There are no limits. Ask and you shall receive. Open yourself for a water-fall of Grace in your life. It's all there. You just need to clear the space and ask.

Climb the mountains and get their good tidings.
Nature's peace will flow into you as sunshine flows into trees.
The winds will blow their own freshness into you,
and the storms their energy,
while care will drop off like autumn leaves.
JOHN MUIR

I INTEND TO CLEAR THE SPACE AND ASK.

I accept that I have the gift of free will... *I relinquish* false beliefs of scarcity and separa-tion... *I dream of* being aware of Nature's gift of healing and abundance... *With peace and love I intend to* be open to receiving Earth's good tidings... *I am grateful* to restore myself by being open to the cleansing effects of our Mother's angels of Air, Light, Water and Fire, *I am.*

We eventually learn that emotional closure is our own action.
We can be responsible for it.
In any moment,
we can choose to open or to close.
DAVID DEIDA

REFLECTIONS ON GIVING FREELY… I yearn to bloom. I yearn to open in beautiful splendor. I yearn to open like a gorgeous flower that blooms with exquisite beauty in the sunlight for all to experience. The flowers give of themselves freely. They experience no pain as they give to all who come to receive the Earth's bounty through them.

The bloomings are exquisite. There is no suffering. In their openness to giving, they cannot be taken from.

The simplicity of it is this:
give everything you have to give
in every moment,
completely.
DAVID DEIDA

I INTEND TO BE GENEROUS.

I accept that the Love that flows through my heart is endless… *I relinquish* fears of exhausting myself from too much giving… *I dream of* being an outlet for Love… *With peace and love I intend to* accept all who come to me… *I am grateful* for the gift of sharing Love with one another, *I am.*

We have all a better guide in ourselves,
if we would attend to it,
that any other person can be.
JANE AUSTEN

REFLECTIONS ON WHAT I AM DRAWN TO... I wish to honor the yearnings... the pulls... that which I am drawn to. I wish to recognize these sensations as Guidance. I wish to honor the Guidance.

Often my head gets in the way. Analyzing and judging whether it be right or wrong.

I choose to live from my being... honoring the subtle, or sometimes not so subtle Yearnings. I intend to recognize the Yearnings as tiny creations striving to come forth into the world.

I did not know I was on a search for the passionate aliveness that I found.
I only knew I was lonely and lost,
and that something was drawing me deeper
beneath the surface of my life in search of meaning.
There is a hunger in people to touch those depths;
to know that our lives are sacred;
that our hearts are truly capable of love.
It is a yearning to be all that we can be.
A longing for what is real.
ANNE HILLMAN, AUTHOR OF
"THE DANCING ANIMAL WOMAN: A CELEBRATION OF LIFE"

I INTEND TO HONOR THE YEARNINGS.

I accept that Yearnings are sacred... *I relinquish* fears of separation that prevent me from perceiving Guidance... *I dream of* having the sensitivity to recognize Guidance... *I dream of* recognizing when fears have returned... *With peace and love I intend to* dance through life guided by the gentle pushes and pulls of my invisible dance partner... *I am grateful* to honor Guidance, *I am.*

"But I will restore you to health and heal your wounds," declares the LORD.

JEREMIAH 30:17

𝓡EFLECTIONS ON OUR HEALING... As I Heal I am becoming aware that I don't do so in isolation. As we Heal we do so together. All is One.

All that live now. All that have come before us. The Healing comes and affects the whole.

I sense that I carry the pain of women that have come before me. I carry the pain that has been transferred through generations.

The memories of experiences where there was an unawareness of Love. I wish to forgive the past. I wish to live with Acceptance. I wish to transform the pain. I wish to only perceive Love, Truth. I wish to let the illusion of the rest fall away into nothingness. Join me.

> *If the doors of perception were cleansed*
> *everything would appear to man as it is:*
> *Infinite.*
> WILLIAM BLAKE

I INTEND TO PERCEIVE ONLY LOVE.

I accept that humanity has lived largely from a state of illusion... *I relinquish* judging myself and others for our lack of Awareness... *I dream of* humanity waking up from the dream... *With peace and love I intend to* do my part of the work that is necessary to live with Awareness and Forgiveness... *I am grateful* to be a part of this Great Transformation, *I am*.

To be a star, you must shine your own light, follow your own path,
and don't worry about the darkness,
for that is when the stars shine brightest.
NAPOLEON HILL

EFLECTIONS ON FLIPPING THE SWITCH... I want to turn on the Light in myself. Permanently. So how do I turn on the Light? I intend to participate in Creating with Love by being healthy: mind, body and spirit. By having a healthy mind, clearing up the lower realm thoughts, there is the space to perceive Inspirations, the seeds for creation. When I am physically healthy, I am inclined to intend for these Inspirations to be out of a natural state of well-being, a faithful spirit. When my body is healthy, I have the strength to back up my intentions with a great amount of unwavering attention. I'm not inclined to lose focus from being distracted by disease and discomfort.

Sometimes I forget the Truth and I fall back into fearful expectation and judgment. I fail to follow the Guidance with faith from knowing that the intentions are manifesting in their own perfect time. I forget to follow my bliss knowing that I am guided by my feelings, my awareness of Guidance. Good feelings are feedback that I am cooperating; negative feelings like tension and agitation are Guidance that I am acting against creation.

I've fluctuated back and forth between the Truth of Creating with Love and the suffering from chaos. I'm ready to be permanently Connected. Now that I have a glimpse of what can be, I feel a responsibility to stay focused and be a source of Love and Healing. I intend to live a life free of judgment. I intend to live a life free of fearful expectations.

When angels visit us, we do not hear the rustle of wings,
nor feel the feathery touch of the breast of a dove;
but we know their presence by the love they create in our hearts.
MARY BAKER EDDY

I INTEND TO CREATE WITH LOVE.

I accept my journey thus far... *I relinquish* the habit of falling back into judging... *I dream of* creating with a Peaceful mind and a Loving heart... *With peace and love I intend to* be filled with Grace... *I am grateful* to create with Love by remembering to honor the Guidance, *I am.*

𝓡EFLECTIONS ON THE VIBRATIONS… Everything vibrates. Everything hums. Different things have different frequencies. I wish to be surrounded by an orchestra. A rich variety of vibrations that sing a song with depth.

A hand-made clay pot feels different than a pot that has come off of a factory-mechanized assembly line. It has a different feel because it is different. The energy of the one who formed it resides within it. It has been touched by the energy of a soul. Touched and forever changed.

I go to the fluorescent-lit grocery store filled with lots and lots of packaging and stuff that is hardly food and I feel deflated as I leave. Other stores and outdoor markets display a bounty of food in its natural form. I leave invigorated from the atmosphere. Merely being amongst the food is nourishing. Kind of like a pot of soup simmering on the stove is enough to nourish me without ever taking a sip.

I wish to be aware of my "tuning fork nature." I wish to be aware of the affects of what surrounds me and to steer my vessel wisely towards that which sings to me a sweet song.

I INTEND TO RESONATE WITH JOY.

I accept all that surrounds me… *I relinquish* fears of things that don't feel right… *I dream of* having the wisdom to honor the pulls that draw me towards that which nourishes me… *With peace and love I intend to* remain alert to all that I am a part of… *I am grateful* for growing Awareness, *I am.*

Who are you then?
"I am a part of that power which eternally wills evil
and eternally works good."
JOHANN WOLFGANG VON GOETHE

REFLECTIONS ON THE CHAIN... I find myself affected by what surrounds me. A walk in the woods restores me. Being in the presence of people plagued with low energy blockages affects me. I can feel it. I'm beginning to understand the word repulsed. I am repulsed by negative energy fields. I observe children and their natural tendencies to honor their attraction to all that nourishes them and their repulsion to all that may harm them.

I'm also becoming aware of when people are drawn to or repulsed by me. It's like we feed off of each other. Unfortunately, we don't always crave the healthy energies. Dark energy forms don't crave Love and Compassion, they crave low energies like anger, frustration and resentment. I see that drama feeds the falseness within us.

As we become aware of this pattern, we can stop participating in it. We can literally starve the beast that plagues us. We can cease to feed the 'ick' in each other. I intend to become aware of my own energy and that which surrounds me. As we transform, so too will the entire earth change. All is linked together. Not a long single chain, but a web. Hold my hand, let's do this together.

In this treacherous world nothing is the truth nor a lie.
Everything depends on the color of the crystal
through which one sees it.
PEDRO CALDERON DE LA BARCA

I INTEND TO CHOOSE THAT WHICH INCREASES MY VIBRATIONS.

I accept that we are all vibrating at various frequencies... *I relinquish* fears of abandoning another if I remove myself from that which lowers my vibrations... *I dream of* moving towards that which restores and invigorates me... *I dream of* sensing the vibrations... *With peace and love I intend to* seek out people and circumstances that lift me up... *I am grateful* for life, the pursuit of creating the most beautiful life I can possibly imagine, *I am.*

*The greater danger for most of us
lies not in setting our aim too high and falling short;
but in setting our aim too low,
and achieving our mark.*
MICHELANGELO BUONARROTI

*R*EFLECTIONS ON GETTING OUT OF A RUT... I see a pattern in myself. I deny myself pleasures. Then I can feel like a victim over the woes of not getting my way. I seem to be addicted to the lower realm energies created by believing myself to be victimized.

*Grace is given
not to them who speak their faith
but to those who live their faith.*
GREGORY THE THEOLOGIAN

I INTEND TO BE ROOTED TO THE FLOW OF LIFE.

I accept that I have functioned out of fear and out of addictions to low energies... *I relinquish* the fears, the victimization, the resentments, and the judgments... *I relinquish* the fearful patterns that have been in place for generations... *I dream of* seeing the patterns in myself, in my mother, in my sisters, in my grandmother, in all of us... *I dream of* letting them fall... *I dream of* my essence to be of Love... *I dream of* being compassionate towards all of us that have inherited fearful thinking... *With peace and love I intend to* walk gracefully saying yes to a life of Joy... *I am grateful* that I am becoming aware that God intends for me to join in creating the most beautiful life I can possibly imagine, *I am.*

We often miss opportunity
because it's dressed in overalls
and looks like work.
THOMAS EDISON

*R*EFLECTIONS ON RELEASE... Some days I venture out to weed the garlic mustard and I am faced with struggle. The plants hold tight to the earth and the stem breaks away leaving the root intact to grow once again. My efforts of removing it are merely on the surface. Once again the weed will grow.

So it is with the weeds within my being; the grudges, the resentments, the pity. Some days even though I make an attempt to let them go, they hold tight sending their roots deep within me. At best I break off the parts that show.

Today was different. I went out to pull the weeds and they pulled from the ground like I was pulling them from butter. They seemed to surrender to my pull. They seemed to just let go from the earth. Surrender. It's not like we had just had a rain and the ground was soft; no, the ground was hard and dry. The plants just seemed to surrender to my pull.

I wonder... Does our Presence affect what surrounds us? Does our Presence flow out and affect the world? Does what we encounter soften or resist in accordance with ourselves?

Surrender. I've so misunderstood this word. I thought it was weak. But now I know that surrender only happens from a place of Strength and Power disguised by humility.

Without ambition one starts nothing.
Without work one finishes nothing.
The prize will not be sent to you.
You have to win it.
RALPH WALDO EMERSON

I INTEND TO ACKNOWLEDGE MY AFFECT ON OUR WORLD.

I accept that my spirit, my state of Being, affects not only myself, but the whole universe... *I relinquish* all that results in low vibrations... *I dream of* having the gift of Grace... *With peace and love I intend to* be Accepting, Loving, Compassionate, Beautiful, and Kind... *I am grateful* for moments of Truth, *I am.*

Ask, and it will be given you;
Seek, and you will find;
Knock, and it will be opened to you.
JESUS (LUKE 11)

ℛEFLECTIONS ON MY GARDEN OF EDEN... I see so much suffering. So many of us precious souls plagued by so much pain. I want us to reach out, embrace each other, kiss each others' temples and ask God to heal our minds.

I ask for our beings to be cleared of all that obscures us. A cleaning of the slate so that the Power of Love can come through us. From that place we become an outlet in our world for the Love that heals.

One by one let us ask for healing so that we might be vessels of Light in our world. Our Garden of Eden is right here; a gathering of souls making the choice to Live Beautifully, making the choice to live as we are intended.

Those who are happiest
are those who do the most for others.
BOOKER T. WASHINGTON

I INTEND TO ASK FOR HEALING FOR ALL.

I accept our world as it is... *I relinquish* fears of the pain and suffering that surrounds me... *I dream of* having eyes that only see the Light in others... *I dream of* having eyes that only see Truth... *With peace and love I intend to* know that we merely need to ask, seek and knock knowing that our requests will be honored... *I am grateful* for Grace, *I am.*

Lord, make me an instrument of your peace,
Where there is hatred, let me sow love; where there is injury, pardon;
where there is doubt, faith; where there is despair, hope;
where there is darkness, light; where there is sadness, joy;
O Divine Master, grant that I may not so much seek to be consoled as to console;
to be understood as to understand; to be loved as to love.
For it is in giving that we receive; it is in pardoning that we are pardoned;
and it is in dying that we are born to eternal life.

PRAYER OF ST. FRANCIS OF ASSISI

REFLECTIONS ON PICKING UP THE WAND... If I could rename the Prayer of St. Francis of Assisi, I would call it The Prayer of Those Called to be Fairy Godmothers and Fairy Godfathers. Cinderella's fairy godmother was filled with Grace. She was a radiant woman. She showed up in Cinderella's life at the perfect moments when she was in need of a little Divine Intervention. Cinderella's fairy godmother was aware of her powers of transformation and used them for works of Love. She was a good witch. Like St. Francis, she too was a master of transformation. A master of turning darkness into Light.

Oh God, I am grateful...
For letting go of old ways. For becoming magical once again.
Gathering with other wise people,
Wonderful people who are remembering their Truth.
Let us make the world a beautiful place. Let us heal ourselves and each other.
Let us embrace the whole of humanity.
Our magic is our knowing of our ability to transform ourselves.
Our prayers are our spells. Our Love is our wand.
Let us gather and rejoice. Amen!

DORIS WEDIGE

I INTEND TO BE AN INSTRUMENT OF PEACE.

I accept the honor of being a fairy Godmother (father)... *I relinquish* beliefs in thoughts of unworthiness... *I dream of* illuminating darkness... *With peace and love I intend to* be a luminous glow of Light... *I am grateful* for this Joy, I am.

I believe so I can understand.
Saint Augustine

*R*EFLECTIONS ON A 'HIDDEN CLAUSE'... Last night I was watching the movie *The Santa Clause* starring Tim Allen. Suddenly I had ears to hear the Truth within the story. Every hair on my body raised, my throat constricted and tears flowed from my eyes. The Truth had been hidden in a child's story and passed down for generations and I didn't even realize it.

I saw it to be the same Truth that is written of in new age books in the concept of creating by asking, believing and receiving. I saw it to be the same Truth that is written of in the biblical passages. A story of an agreement, a clause made between a masculine figure that we never actually get to see but believe in... A masculine figure that has a joyful love for every girl and boy... A masculine figure that can see our every moment... A father figure that delights in those who are nice rather than naughty... A father figure that commands that for us to enjoy the gifts that He bestows, one must have the childlike innocence of faith... The story of when we cease to believe with the innocent eyes of a child, the magic ceases to be.

Without faith, we are cut off from the joy and the flow of the bounty. Without faith, we cease to hear the ringing of the bells, the messages of truth from our heavenly angels. Santa Claus is a story of joy, a story of faith, a story of magic, a story of endless abundance.

And so I see, the Santa Clause is an agreement between each of us and our Father. As we remember the Truth and Believe, we will be guided by joy and blessed with receiving the most beautiful lives we can possibly imagine.

...is there anything you can't make? ...well just like anything, if you put your mind to it you will, that's how you are.
Scott Wedige

I INTEND TO BELIEVE.

I accept that Truth has been handed down through the ages in stories... *I relinquish* skepticism... *I dream of* us all seeing with the eyes of a child... *With peace and love I intend to* allow the knowing to sink into my bones... *I am grateful* for those who so wisely taught in stories that would be least apt to conjure up resistance, *I am.*

Forgiveness is the economy of the heart...
forgiveness saves the expense of anger,
the cost of hatred,
the waste of spirits.
HANNAH MORE

ℛEFLECTIONS ON MY PAST... I see that I have done my best to survive in a world that is broken in many places. I see that I am ready to go beyond merely survival to being a healing presence. I am ready to embrace a new way of being.

The real voyage of discovery
consists not in seeking new landscapes,
but in having new eyes.
MARCEL PROUST

I INTEND TO LET GO OF JUDGING THE PAST, PRESENT OR FUTURE.

I *accept* that there are consequences to every choice of thought, action and spirit... *I relinquish* believing that I must continue to pay for my sins, to live out the consequences of my choices that were based on false beliefs... *I dream of* seeing the errors that I have committed with Compassion... *With peace and love I intend to* ask for the Healing of my mind when I am aware of falseness, thus freeing me from repeating the same mistakes... *With peace and love I intend to* ask for the undoing of the consequences of my errors... *I am grateful* to be Forgiven, *I am.*

Index of Reflections

Index of Reflections

Made in the USA
Lexington, KY
16 May 2018